Non-Stop Creativity and Innovation

How to generate winning ideas and put them into practice

Non-Stop Creativity and Innovation

How to generate winning ideas and put them into practice

**Fiona McLeod
and
Richard Thomson**

THE McGRAW-HILL COMPANIES

London · Burr Ridge IL · New York · St Louis · San Francisco
Auckland · Bogotá · Caracas · Lisbon · Madrid · Mexico · Milan
Montreal · New Delhi · Panama · Paris · San Juan · São Paulo
Singapore · Sydney · Tokyo · Toronto

Published by McGraw-Hill Professional
Shoppenhangers Road
Maidenhead
Berkshire
SL6 2QL
Telephone: 44 (0) 1628 502 500
Fax: 44 (0) 1628 770 224
Website: www.mcgraw-hill.co.uk

Sponsoring Editor: Elizabeth Robinson
Editorial Assistant: Sarah Wilks
Business Marketing Manager: Elizabeth McKeever
Senior Production Manager: Max Elvey

Produced for McGraw-Hill by Steven Gardiner Ltd
Text design by Steven Gardiner Ltd
Printed and bound in Great Britain by Bell and Bain Ltd, Glasgow
Cover design by Senate Design Ltd

McGraw-Hill

*A Division of The **McGraw-Hill** Companies*

British Library Cataloguing in Publication Data
A catalogue record for this book is available from the British Library

Library of Congress Cataloguing in Publication Data
The Library of Congress data for this book
has been applied for from the Library of Congress

ISBN 0 07 7098867 6

McGraw-Hill books are available at special quantity discounts. Please contact the
Corporate Sales Executive at the above address.

Every effort has been made to trace the copyright owner of the illustration of the clock
designed by Paolo Uccello reproduced on p. 36, but it has not been possible to do so.
However, if the copyright owner would like to contact us we will be happy to make suitable
acknowledgement in any future reprint.

Contents

First Steps

In your work have you ever found yourself imagining how much better it would be if you only had a new product, a new system, a new way of operating? Would you like to be able to find new and inventive ways of doing things in your personal life? Have you ever wanted to find a winning idea for a new business? This book will give you the guidance you need to produce these and other winning ideas, not just once, but as often as you like.

We will take you on a journey of discovery through the creative and innovative process. As you read and work through the activities which we include in each chapter, you will be able to step outside your usual way of looking at things, expand your thinking and generate more new and inventive ideas than you could ever have thought possible. Your self-confidence will grow as your creative skills improve and you become more at ease with your natural creativity. And very importantly, you will be able to turn your new ideas into reality. You'll know what and how to plan and how to persuade people to buy in to your ideas and so help make them happen.

By using these skills you can enhance your experience of the world, push your thinking and be more inventive and productive. Whether you are cooking a meal, planning a garden, designing a room or looking for a new way of tackling an old problem, being able to think creatively and come up with genuinely new ideas will make the results better and the process more enjoyable. Imagine you are looking for a new job, how can you get yourself noticed? Think creatively. What if you've been asked by your boss to present a new product to a client and you don't know where to start? Think creatively. Rather than do what's been done before or a variation of it, think creatively. What's in it for you? More enjoyment, more interest, better work, winning ideas . . . success.

Throughout the book you'll learn about and use the Uccello™ Process, a step-by-step guide to generating and implementing new ideas, which we developed as a result of having worked for more than twenty years with people in the fields of business and culture who are consistently creative.

Before you embark on your journey, however, here are some **frequently asked questions** about creativity and innovation. See if you can answer them. (You will find our answers on pages 10–13.)

1 Isn't creativity mostly about art and being artistic?
2 Do we only use the right side of our brain when we're being creative?
3 What difference does it make whether or not an organisation is creative as long as there is a market for whatever it does?
4 I get my ideas out of the blue, when I'm in the shower, or just relaxing. How can I come up with ideas whenever I want or need them?
5 I don't think I'm a creative person, is it possible to learn how to be more creative?
6 How can I motivate people to be creative at work?
7 Is being creative easy once you've learned how to do it?
8 What does thinking out of the box mean?
9 I've got some ideas that I think could make our company more efficient and successful, but how can I get people to listen to them?
10 Is taking a systematic approach to creativity not a contradiction?
11 What is the difference between creativity and innovation?

How did you do? We hope that some of your questions have been answered and perhaps we have dispelled some common myths surrounding creativity and innovation.

Everyone is capable of being creative. We are all born with an inventiveness of spirit. If you watch very young children and see how they interact with the world around them, there is an excitement and a complete lack of inhibition as everyday objects are imaginatively and magically transformed into something different and new. Everything is a game and an adventure. As we grow up, however, this spontaneous enjoyment of creativity becomes tempered by social values, personal inhibitions, the need to 'fit in' and so on. We look at the world through adult eyes and we end up using only a fraction of our creative potential. Even when we *are* being creative in our day-to-day life, for example, when we're cooking or gardening or pursuing our hobbies, we tend not to think of these as 'creativity' and when it comes to being creative in work, we feel even more hesitant and poorly equipped. Sometimes, we're held back by lack of self-confidence, lack of knowledge of where to start, lack of support by our bosses or perhaps just lack of opportunity. By using the Uccello™ Process to develop and practise our skills we can regain some of that openness we had as children and rediscover how being creative, generating new ideas about any subject is challenging, it's fun and it makes us feel good about ourselves. Turning those ideas into reality is a different kind of challenge and, when we succeed, the sense of achievement is extraordinary.

In our work, if we're prepared to question our preconceptions and look at things from different perspectives we are likely to find that there are systems, methods, products and services that, if we were starting over, we wouldn't even introduce let alone work with. There's probably a more efficient, more cost-effective, more interesting product or way of working which, if we only had the time to think about it, we would develop and use. How often have you heard, 'if it ain't broke don't fix it'? And how many systems and products which you use in your work, while they aren't broken, could be much better? We learn to accommodate the shortcomings of systems and processes because it's sometimes quicker and almost always easier than trying to find a new and better way. Imagine if it was the normal, expected thing that everyone in the organisation regularly took the time to find new ways of doing their job. Think about the benefits for the organisation and for the people in it – up-to-date systems and processes, products that give a competitive edge, staff who are engaged by what they do and are highly motivated. This isn't Utopia, it is a practical possibility if people are given the opportunity to develop and apply their creativity.

Likewise, on a personal level, if we're prepared to do things differently we might, for example, use our creative skills to bring ourselves to the attention of potential employers, we might seek out new ways of developing ourselves intellectually and physically, we might rethink our house or garden or we might design our ideal vacation. If we can learn to develop our creativity there is no limit to the ideas we can generate or the areas of our lives we can apply it to. We must start, however, by challenging our existing thinking and questioning what we do and how we do it. Only then is it possible to move away from doing things the same old way just because that's how we've always done them.

When we look at the pattern of our day-to-day lives it's surprising to discover just how much repetition and sameness there is about what we think and how we spend our time. Think about your day from the time you wake up until you go to bed and consider how many activities are repetitious and follow the same pattern day after day: getting out of bed, showering, dressing, opening your mail, travelling to work, and so on – there aren't too many original thoughts there. Just how much time do you spend carrying out activities that are *not* part of this repeat pattern and how many genuinely new thoughts do you have in a day? If your life is like most other people's then the majority of your thoughts will be the same from one day to the next. So it's hardly surprising that challenging our perceptions, questioning the way we think feels uncomfortable and can be hard work. This book is a guide, an operator's manual if you like, for doing just that. Learning how to use the Uccello™ Process will help you to think outside of the constraints placed on us by the pattern of everyday life.

This manual of creativity and innovation is designed to be inter-active. You can work through it from the beginning, following and learning the steps in the Uccello™ Process or you can dip into it to find an answer to specific questions or to trigger a new thought. To help you find information quickly and enable you to navigate around the book we have used the following symbols:

Activity

 When you see this symbol, there is an exercise or activity designed to open up your thinking and develop your skills in creativity and innovation. Sometimes the activities are mental, sometimes physical and always fun.

When you see this symbol there is a useful piece of information, which will enhance your knowledge of creativity and innovation. These include research findings and interesting facts about creative thinking and innovative practice in real situations.

When you see this symbol you will find a hint or an observation which, if you apply it, will put you on the fast track to developing and building your creative ability and your skills as an innovator.

Each chapter deals with one of the steps in the Uccello™ Process. We explain each one fully and the activities will give you the opportunity to look at things from some very different perspectives and to experience creativity and innovation in action. Starting with Chapter 2 when you work on defining what you want to generate ideas about, until you reach Chapter 8 where you make a plan for implementing those ideas, you will work with real material which you choose and which you can apply in your work or your personal life. The activities are designed for you to work on alone and, in Chapter 10, we will show you how each can be adapted for use with groups and teams. They can be repeated as often as you want.

Creativity and innovation

In the Uccello™ Process we make a clear distinction between creativity and innovation. We define creativity as:

Combining previously unconnected ideas, information and elements to make something new.

And innovation as:

The process of turning new ideas into practical reality.

Throughout the book we will build on this idea of combining as the essence of creativity. Once you've practised this, you will find yourself experiencing the pleasure and excitement of inventing new things and you'll find that even the way you think changes as your skills develop. To demonstrate what we mean and to get your imagination working, try this short combining activity.

Activity 1.1 Combining

Working with the following items, a *hat*, a *clock*, a *fish* and a *newspaper*, invent a new game. There's only one rule: you must use all four items and nothing else. Let your imagination go!

How did you do? Did you find it easy or was it a bit of a struggle because you kept evaluating and questioning whether your idea was any good? Did you pursue your ideas even when they were a bit unusual or out of the ordinary? If you did, well done! You may have found that many of your ideas were variations on games that are familiar to you. In our workshops we've had any number of variations on bat and ball games, but we've also had the more unusual including, on one memorable occasion, competitive fish wrapping. The key is to keep pushing the combinations until new and more imaginative connections are made.

Using the Uccello™ Process will help you to avoid judging your ideas too early because it includes, at step 7, the opportunity to evaluate. We find that when people know they will have the chance to sift and filter their ideas they become freer and more willing to entertain those unusual and more 'off-the-wall' notions. There follows an overview of the Uccello™ Process and a brief summary of each step.

The Uccello™ Process starts with us identifying what we want to generate ideas about; we define our purpose. This first step acts as

The Uccello™ Process For Non-Stop Creativity

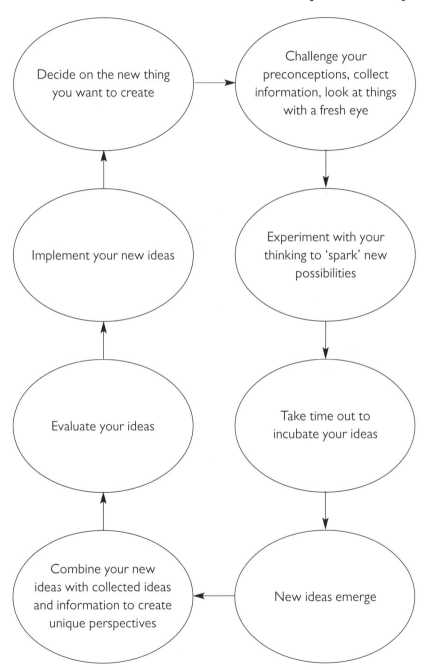

Source: Fiona McLeod and Richard Thomson, 1997.

the driver for the whole process because, having thought carefully about what it is we really want, we set up a tension between what we have now and that desired future. It is this tension that pushes the creative process forward and gives it momentum. Our purpose is always about finding something *new* and we word it carefully in order to give focus and direction to our ideas generation. In Chapter 2 you will prepare your own purpose which you will use throughout the book as your focus for all the activities.

Having decided on our purpose we must challenge our preconceptions and mindsets and in doing so we prepare the ground for new ideas. We need to work with a wide range of information and experiences which will then form the building blocks we use to generate ideas. People who are consistently creative, those people we hear and read about who produce winning ideas again and again, are avid collectors of information. They seek out new experiences and maintain a broad range of interests. When we collect information and look at things from different perspectives we may find ideas occurring to us about how we can achieve our purpose. At this stage, however, we need to exercise patience and hold onto our ideas so that we can add to them and develop them further. In Chapter 3 you will find out how inquisitiveness and curiosity are ideal attributes for the creative person and you will be able to use the activities to open your mind and your senses to new perspectives and experiences.

The next step in the process gives us the opportunity to use tools and techniques to experiment with our thinking. By using techniques such as 'Random input' and 'Metaphor' we can provoke different ways of thinking and spark off new ideas. In Chapter 4 you will use a number of methods for playing with and breaking out of your thinking in relation to your purpose. You will see your ideas grow and develop and become richer and more adventurous as you experiment with them.

In Step 4 of the Uccello™ Process, we give our unconscious mind the opportunity to make connections our conscious mind wouldn't normally make and, as a result, even more ideas are produced. In Chapter 5, you will try out techniques for relaxing and slowing down your mind in order to dip into your unconscious.

Now we come to combining, the key to creativity. Combining the ideas we've had with other, unconnected ideas and information makes for unexpected and original results. In our workshops, at this point in the process, it is quite common for groups of four people to generate anywhere between 50 and a 100 ideas in relation to their purpose in not much more than half an hour. In Chapter 6 you will read about how many of the most successful inventors, innovators and entrepreneurs have used combining and you will have the opportunity to make your own connections and combinations to generate ideas that will meet your purpose,

Because the Uccello™ Process is designed as a practical tool and generating ideas is only part of what we need to be able to do, we don't stop there. When we use the Process, by this stage, we have generated many ideas in relation to our purpose. Now it's time to sort and filter those ideas so that we have a manageable number to work with. The next step in the process, therefore, is evaluation. This step is vital, not only because it allows us the chance to reduce the number of ideas we will go on to work with, but also because knowing we have a specific opportunity to evaluate goes a long way to stopping us prejudging and limiting our thinking as we go along. We won't, therefore, throw out potentially good ideas just because we think they sound a bit crazy! In Chapter 7 you will have the opportunity to use a specially designed decision-making tool to help you organise your thoughts and sort your ideas.

Finally, having evaluated our ideas against a set of predetermined criteria, we can select which one we want to implement first. This is where creativity becomes innovation and our idea becomes a practical reality. Before this can happen, however, and to give ourselves the best chance of success, we must plan. We need to take into account all the people who will be affected by our idea if it were to be implemented. We need to be prepared to present it to these people and to those others whose support we need. Whether you are an entrepreneur, a factory worker or senior executive, planning the implementation of your idea will increase your chances of getting people to buy in to it and make it a reality. In Chapter 8, you will find out about how to make a plan that will give you the best chance of success. You will learn about Ideas champions and how they can help you. You will find out about how to manage getting buy-in and how to minimise resistance. And, working with the idea you have selected in Chapter 7, you'll make a real plan for its implementation.

As you can see, we designed the Uccello™ Process as a step-by-step sequence and to some extent the creative and innovative process is sequential. After all, you must come up with an idea before you can implement it. The Uccello™ Process is not a formula, however, and you follow the sequence only as far as you need to, going back and forth through the steps, repeating them as the need arises.

Before you embark on your journey into creativity and innovation remember, your mind is like a parachute, it only works when it's open. Working through this book you will arrive at your destination a more creative and innovative person, so enjoy the journey and don't forget to smell the flowers.

Answers to frequently asked questions

1 Artists are creative as are scientists, engineers, business people, entrepreneurs, travel agents, customer service staff, bankers, everyone. Creativity does not belong exclusively to the world of artists and the arts; we are all creative in our personal and our work lives even though we don't always recognise it.

2 It is a common misconception that only one side of our brain deals with creative thoughts. It has been said that the left side of the brain operates coldly and logically while the right side is our imaginative side. But experiments done as recently as 1996 (Fink and Marshal, *Nature*, 382, p. 626. Source: *New Scientist*, 163 (2193), 03/07/1999, p. 26) show clearly that the difference between the two halves of the brain is more about their style of working, with the left side being more focused on detail and the right side more focused on the bigger, background picture. So, in fact, we use both sides of our brain at different times when we are being creative.

3 Change is the normal state of affairs in the twenty-first century so organisations must be flexible, responsive and

prepared to think differently. Even those organisations that have a unique product or provide a service which no other organisation offers must continually seek new approaches and methods of working if they're to stay ahead. Also, people like working for organisations that are at the leading edge. They thrive in a work environment that provides a challenge and offers them the chance to be creative and innovative in their own right.

4   Early views of creativity were that it resulted from divine intervention or cosmic forces. The reason you get your ideas when you are relaxed is because in this state, your unconscious makes connections which your fully alert mind does not. However, while these new ideas may appear to come out of the blue, they are always connected with something you have been thinking about that has set up a creative tension which your conscious and unconscious mind has worked to resolve. Creativity isn't about bringing something out of nothing. It means using existing ideas, information and elements to produce a new combination. If ideas can be said to involve a 'Eureka' moment, a moment of illumination, it is at the point where this new pattern, this new arrangement emerges. In this book we will introduce you to the Uccello™ Process which replicates what happens in your brain when you are being creative. You will learn how to use this process not only to help you develop your natural creativity so that you can generate genuinely new ideas in a focused way, but you will also be able to plan for their implementation.

5   Everyone has the ability to be creative. You don't have to have some kind of 'specialness' to be able to think and act creatively. Being creative has to do with bringing into existence a new combination of elements that did not previously exist and this description applies to any human product. If we know how the creative process works we can develop our skill and, with practice, become adept at using it.

6   People are most creative when they feel motivated by the interest, enjoyment and challenge associated with a particular task. The act of being creative is an intrinsic motivator in itself,

i.e. it provides 'a strong internal desire to do something based on interests and passions' (Theresa M. Amabile, 'How to kill creativity', *Harvard Business Review On Breakthrough Thinking*, HBS Press, 1999). If you establish an environment where people have the space and opportunity to generate new ideas they will do so. Curiously, external rewards for creative ideas produce fewer and poorer quality ideas than if people are just given the chance to be creative.

7 Some aspects of the ideas-generating process are lighter and easier than others. Experimenting with our thinking can be a lot of fun and when we start combining information and ideas to make something new it can be a really enjoyable challenge. We expend a lot of energy as we push and stretch our thinking and produce more and more ideas. However, changing the way we think, keeping our options open and suspending judgement so that we can add even more information and ideas to those we've already had can be hard work. When we move from generating ideas to implementing them we need to persevere and may have to work very hard in order to see our ideas become a reality. The Wright brothers, for example, tried 805 times before they achieved sustained flight.

8 In day-to-day life we see only what we want to see. Partly because of the way the brain works and partly because of a need for stability, we filter out information, ignore alternatives and interpret things in terms of our existing worldview. We channel the information we receive in the same way that we've done in the past and so our thoughts and ideas become 'boxed'. We need something to stop us from only thinking in a straight line. In order to think 'out of the box' we need to introduce something different and entirely unconnected to provoke new ways of thinking.

9 Although innovation can begin with individual creativity, teams possess a range of abilities, skills and experience all of which can be drawn on successfully to translate our creative ideas into innovative practice. Most major innovative breakthroughs involve collaboration and including the team at an early stage will help them to buy in. The collaboration can

take different forms: it might involve individuals co-creating or team members playing complementary roles such as facilitator or Ideas champion. Introducing new ideas into an organisation is about bringing the new, the different, the untried or untested into a given situation. It challenges the status quo and, as such, is likely to be met with more resistance than other forms of change. To innovate successfully we need to plan in detail how we will introduce our new idea and we need to persevere to make it happen.

10 The creative process is essentially the same whether it is concerned with day-to-day problem solving or highly specialised scientific discovery. It is made up of a series of steps and by understanding, practising and following these we can develop our ability and, like any other learned skill, we begin to do it without thinking. As this happens and our skill improves so the number and quality of ideas generated increases.

11 The essential difference is that creativity is about generating ideas and innovation is about implementing them. We define creativity as, 'Combining previously unconnected ideas, information and elements to make something new'. Innovation on the other hand is related to introducing our ideas into the world and we define this as, 'The process of turning new ideas into practical reality'. This includes introducing ideas which may not be new in themselves but which previously have never been applied in this way or in this situation or context.

2

Decide What You Want to Create

Creativity is about bringing together elements including information, thoughts and ideas and combining them to make something new. Generating creative ideas can be like walking around a maze looking for a way out, where we need to explore wrong turnings as well as right ones if we are to end up with truly creative outcomes. In work, the need for quick results often leads to ideas being generated that are not truly new; they're amendments or alterations to what already exists. Faced with the usual kind of direct incentives most managers and businesses employ, it's not really surprising that we look for the shortest, straightest route out of the maze. For really creative ideas to emerge what's needed is time and space to explore the maze and to experience all its twists and turns.

Not only do we need the conditions that allow us to explore the creative maze, it is also helpful to have a clear and understandable process to follow. For many of us our search for something new, whether that's a new way of tackling an old problem or a completely new invention, is fairly random. We have a notion of what it is we want and we hope that an idea will come to us. Sure enough, if we wait long enough one usually does. To get a good idea we seem to have to wait for that 'Eureka' moment to happen. We depend on our unconscious to make connections for us because we're unsure how to enlist our conscious mind to help us. The Uccello™ Process, however, allows us to use both our conscious as well as our unconscious mind to the full and provides us with a way in which we can generate ideas so that we don't have to wait for that 'Eureka' moment. It helps us to develop our creativity and leads to more unique ideas.

The Uccello™ Process For Non-Stop Creativity

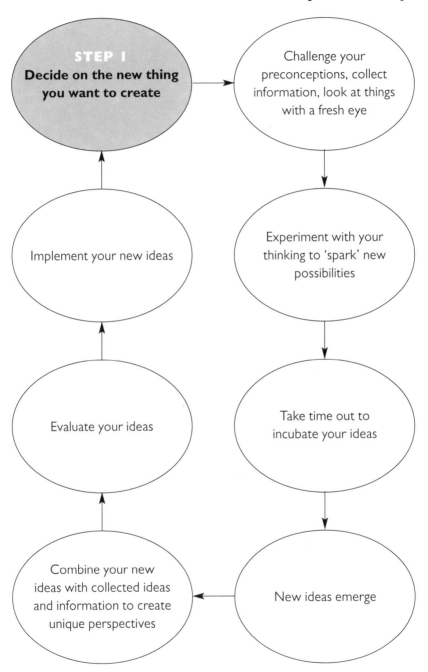

STEP I
Decide on the new thing you want to create

Challenge your preconceptions, collect information, look at things with a fresh eye

Implement your new ideas

Experiment with your thinking to 'spark' new possibilities

Evaluate your ideas

Take time out to incubate your ideas

Combine your new ideas with collected ideas and information to create unique perspectives

New ideas emerge

Source: Fiona McLeod and Richard Thomson, 1997.

Fast Fact *Creativity is an intrinsic motivator*

 Given the opportunity and 'climate' within which we can be creative, we will work to generate potentially winning ideas and we do so because we want to not because someone is offering us a reward.

Those ideas that come, apparently from nowhere, are caused by the tension that builds up in our mind when there is a difference between what we have now and what we want. That tension, that niggle in the back of our mind is usually something we've been puzzling about. It could be something that isn't working properly or we know there must be a better way to do it, perhaps it's something new altogether. That persistent 'itch' in the back of our mind is the thing that acts as the spark to ignite our imagination. When we are puzzling like this we might wake up in the morning with an idea about how to get what it is we want or perhaps an idea will come to us when we are in the shower or driving to work. This is because, while we were asleep or relaxing and probably not even thinking about it, our unconscious has been brought into play and has made connections which have produced a possible answer to what was niggling us. There is a tension created between our dissatisfaction with the way things are now and how we would like them to be and it's this tension that is the powerful catalyst for creative thought. The longer the puzzle remains unresolved, the more the tension builds and the more ideas we produce.

True creativity focuses on what is genuinely new. Many people talk about and tend to think of creativity in relation to problem solving, however, if we do this, our attention will mainly be on doing the same thing but in a different way. Of course it depends on what you mean by problem solving, but if you focus on finding new, possibly completely different ways of doing something, you will avoid stifling the more radical thoughts that are essential to true creativity.

The mere formulation of a problem is more often essential than its solution, which may be merely a matter of mathematical or experimental skill. To raise new problems from a new angle requires creative imagination and marks real advances in science.

Albert Einstein

The first step in the Uccello™ Process is to identify our purpose, the thing we want to create and this sets up the tension that is the essential driver for the creative process.

How to write a purpose

When we talk about *purpose* in the Uccello™ Process we are referring to the new thing we want, the resolution to the puzzle that's been bothering us.

Because creativity is about generating new ideas and not simply about solving problems, it's important that we focus our purpose on the future. We do this by stating clearly what the *new* thing is that we want to create. Why new? Because by stating that we want something new rather than merely changing or enhancing something that exists already we open up our mind to different possibilities. If we say we only want a *better* way of doing something we run the risk of limiting our thinking to doing it essentially the same way but with modifications. Maybe there is a completely different way of doing it altogether . . .

This can be difficult for people to accept but our insistence on focusing on the *new* is the best way to generate truly creative ideas.

Hot Tip   *Don't evaluate too soon*

 At work when you want to create something new you may find people very resistant. They would rather you modified what was there already, or even better, just leave things as they are. At this stage in the creative process it is vital that you don't let this stop you. There is plenty of time for evaluating your ideas and for involving others in their implementation when you get to that stage in the Uccello™ Process. Evaluating too soon, either because of your own inhibitions or because of what you imagine others might think, is one of the main reasons many new ideas never see the light of day.

We always recommend writing a purpose down. This is to help clarify what we mean so as to ensure that anyone else involved shares our understanding and, not least, so that we don't forget what we are generating ideas about! It's also a good idea to think carefully about your choice of words to ensure they are future oriented and state clearly what it is you want to create.

When you're describing your purpose, if you always start with the words 'I want a new . . .' you will find it easier to escape more of the same. For example, if you wanted to generate ideas about, say, lighting a room and you begin by stating that your purpose is 'I want a new way to light a room' you are likely to produce more interesting results than if you said 'I want a better way to light a room'. By focusing on the new we move away from what we know and are familiar with. Try it and see how many novel ways you can find to light a room. You will find our ideas on page 25 of this chapter. You may think many of them are far-fetched but at this stage that is less important than simply generating ideas. Remember, you will get a chance to evaluate later.

Here are some examples of purposes our clients have worked with to generate ideas:

A client who wanted to develop ideas about how to make his building sites safer and more productive places to work said:

'I want a new way to create the site of the future.'

The result was 200 ideas relating to every aspect of the sites and went far beyond just safety and productivity.

Another client who wanted to improve the motivation in his team came up with a purpose that was much more developed than his first thoughts, it was:

*'I want a new way to encourage people to **want** to work together.'*

The result was over 150 ideas that addressed not only people's attitudes but also the whole environment in which they worked and which contributed to their motivation.

On a more personal level, someone we know was fairly unhappy in her work but, because she had been doing the same kind of thing all her professional life, she felt she couldn't do anything else. Besides, she needed to maintain her level of income so that she could continue to go on the exotic holidays that were her main motivation. Her purpose was:

'I want a new way to work and be able to travel.'

The result was over 70 ideas for new careers one of which involved her becoming self-employed and working abroad. It may seem fairly obvious but asking herself to think of *new* ways to get what she wanted (to still be able to travel and to get back to enjoying her work) helped her to think 'out of the box' she had put herself in.

Your purpose statement should:

- say what it is you want without trying to give an answer
- start with the words 'I WANT A NEW . . .'

Example

For instance, say you would like to be able to tell the time at any moment. Compare these two purpose statements and see which one you think meets the above criteria:

(a) 'I WANT A NEW way to see my watch all the time'.
(b) 'I WANT A NEW way to be able to tell the time 24 hours a day without having to look for a clock or watch'.

Statement (a) starts with the correct words but fails because it limits us to only thinking about a watch. Statement (b) is so much more open, it leaves us free to think more widely and is, therefore, more likely to produce creative results.

Before you try the next activity, you might find it useful to 'warm up' with these simple exercises.

Which of these purpose statements is likely to produce the most creative results? (See below for our thoughts on which ones work best.)

1 I want a new way to organise my time so that I can spend more time in my garden.
  or
2 I want a new way to relax.

3 I want a new way to give comprehensive feedback to staff and to get feedback from them.
  or
4 I want a new way to do staff performance reviews.

5 I want a new way to improve my golf swing.
  or
6 I want a new way to reduce my golf handicap.

Our answers to the 'warm up' purposes are:

- If the reason you want to spend more time in your garden is to help you to feel more relaxed, then purpose 2 is likely to produce more creative results than purpose 1 because it doesn't limit your thinking. Of course, if your aim is to grow prize-winning vegetables then purpose 1 is the one for you!
- Purpose 3 introduces the possibility that there may be other, perhaps better, ways of reviewing staff performance than the usual, systematic staff performance review.
- Purpose 6 goes to the real reason for improving your golf swing, presumably to improve your overall golfing ability, and there might be a way of doing that which involves more than just your golf swing.

How did you do? Do you see how the way we word our purpose makes a difference to how we think about it?

Now you will write a purpose statement of your own. This should be related to your work and you should keep a note of it as you will use it in the Activities throughout the book.

Activity *2.1 Writing a purpose*

 Step I
Think about the new thing you want.

Step 2
Once you have a reasonably clear picture of your desired future, try writing down a 'purpose statement' starting with the words, 'I want a new . . .' Do this without thinking too much and see what results you get.

Step 3

Read your statement over and ask yourself:

- Is it future oriented?
- If this purpose was achieved, would it remove the 'niggle'?
- Does your statement really ask for something new and not just a modification of something that already exists?

Step 4

Think about the future once whatever it is you want has become a reality. Try to put yourself in that imaginary future. What is different? How do you feel? What are other people doing? (See Visualising below.)

Step 5

Revise your statement to make it as open as possible without losing focus.

You will probably need to experiment with writing purpose statements until you become comfortable with it, but practising will pay off.

Visualising

Visualising really just means thinking about the future as if it had already happened, daydreaming if you like. If this sounds a bit unrealistic and maybe daydreaming is something you never do or is something your boss wouldn't let you get away with, suspend judgement for a moment or two and consider this very effective tool for helping you realise your goals and objectives.

In our work with clients we use visualising in many different ways including helping them with issues such as strategic planning and decision making. You can use it in any area where you need to think ahead and anticipate what might happen in the future. Not everyone finds it easy to think into the future in this way, but with some assistance, anyone can do it. Visualising can be used to remove some of the unconscious barriers that we put in the way of striving for something we want. Imagining a future in which our goal has been achieved, seeing ourselves with what it is we want and visualising ourselves enjoying all the benefits that accrue as a result, creates an image that can exert a very strong attraction that almost pulls us towards it.

The need to be practical means that we tend to think about *how* we will achieve something almost as soon as we have thought about *what* it is we want to achieve. It's thinking about how we'll do it that is problematic because this focuses our attention on the difficulties in making it happen with the result that we don't try new ways and we continue to do things as they have always been done. We tell ourselves, 'It'll never work' so we make less effort. We don't make plans for how to remove obstacles, we make assumptions about what other people think and how they will react with the result, of course, that nothing happens and our self-fulfilling prophecy comes true.

You either believe you can or believe you can't, either way you'll be right.

Henry Ford

The alternative is to think it *will* happen, to believe you can *make* it happen. Then visualise it and see yourself and everyone around you enjoying the benefits. This only works if you don't put any obstructions in the way; if you don't allow yourself to think of the reasons why it won't work. We're not being unrealistic in saying this, we know the difficulties and realities of introducing new things. By using the Uccello™ Process, however, we ensure that there is a time and place for considering the practicalities of innovating and steps 7 and 8 in the Process deal specifically with this. At this crucial stage in the creative-thinking process, however, we need to adopt a more positive frame of mind and to think solely about what it is we want to happen. Using visualising in conjunction with thinking about our purpose can make it easier to write a purpose statement and make the content richer and more comprehensive. It can also be very helpful in clarifying exactly what it is we really want.

Activity *2.2 Visualising*

Variation I

Step I

Imagine it is your habit to keep a journal in which you record your thoughts and what's happened throughout each day. What you are going to do is to record a day in the future when your purpose has been achieved.

Step 2

Select a date when you think that your purpose will have been achieved and will have been in place for some time. Make sure the date you choose is no more than 2 years away. You needn't be too specific about your date, for example, 'it's mid January next year' is close enough.

Step 3

Try to imagine your life at that time in order to put your journal in context. For example, how old will you be? If you have a partner and/or children how old will they be? Where might you be living? Will you be doing the same job or a different one?

Step 4

Imagine your purpose having been achieved.

Step 5

Write down, as if you were writing a journal, what your day has been like on the date in the future you selected and what has been happening to you. Record everything including your feelings and the reactions of other people. For example, how did the new things that are going on make you feel? What did people do differently? How did they behave?

Step 6

The result should be a short essay entitled 'What I did today' and is likely to make interesting reading.

The impact of visualising can be very powerful. One of our clients used our technique of writing a journal to crystallise her vision in the early stages of her business career. She made many plans but never lost sight of that early vision. Now her business has grown five-fold and she is able to consider leaving her senior management to run the operation so she can devote time to her new family which is exactly what she visualised.

Variation 2

If you find it difficult to write a short journal entry such as we describe above, you might find it easier to follow the same steps but, instead of writing, you might tell your story to a friend or colleague whom you trust and who will play the role of listener and facilitator. In this role he or she will ask you questions to draw out your thinking and check understanding. This person must not contradict or disagree with anything you say, their role is purely to help you clarify your thinking. If you are using this method, the facilitator might write notes for you to take away or you might record your story on tape.

Variation 3

As above but recorded on tape with no facilitator.

Variation 4

Step 1

Get clear in your mind what it is you want to happen (your purpose).

Step 2

Select a date in the future by which you think your purpose could be achieved.

Step 3

Imagine you are sitting in front of a television watching a video tape entitled, 'My life once I have achieved my purpose'.

Step 4

Imagine watching your video all the way through; picture all the scenes and the dialogue.

Step 5

Now try playing your video backwards, from the end to the beginning. This can help you focus on the details and fix them in your mind.

Step 6

If you want to, write down the key points from your video, but this is probably not necessary as your memory of your video is likely to be very clear.

Variation 5

Step 1

Get clear in your mind what it is you want to happen (your purpose).

Step 2

Imagine a house and get a picture of the outside of the house clear in your mind.

Step 3

Each room in your house contains an aspect of your life once your purpose has been achieved, i.e. your home life, social life, work life, family, ambitions, aspirations and so on.

Step 4

Now picture yourself walking through the front door of your house and entering the first room.

Step 5

See yourself in that area of your life once your purpose has been achieved. What is happening? How do you feel?

Step 6

Once you have spent enough time in the first room, continue to explore your house, room by room, seeing each aspect in turn.

Step 7

As with Variation 4 above, your memory of the content of your house will remain with you and you can revisit it at any time.

If you've worked through these activities you should now have a good idea not only of what you want to create, but also how to start the process of getting this purpose clear in your mind. In the next few chapters we will work with you to develop your thinking and your ideas.

Our thoughts on how you could light a room

Glass walls, glass ceiling, curtains containing fibre optics, night vision glasses, wall coverings containing a solar-powered light source, thousands of fireflies in a glass container.

3
Curiouser and Curiouser

Step 2 of the Uccello™ Process

Now that you have your purpose and you've looked into the future to see what your new world will look like once you've achieved that purpose, you have set out on your creative journey.

In Chapter 1 we discovered how a new idea is formed. It comes from putting together existing ideas, pieces of information and experiences to make something new. Now we're going to look at how, by opening up our mind and providing it with the raw material, the building blocks to work with, we can give it the best chance of making those new and potentially unique combinations. This is what Step 2 of the Uccello™ Process is about; it's the preparation stage of the creative process.

Imagine you were going to paint a door. How would you go about it? Would you immediately open a pot of paint and start painting? If you did, the result is likely to be a mess. To do the job properly you would have to prepare the door first and the more thorough your preparation, the better the final result. You would begin by sanding it to remove the old paint, you'd brush it down to clean it, then undercoat it and, only once the surface was ready, would you apply the paint. Most of us at some time have been guilty of poor preparation and hurried application and have paid the price.

Being creative is very similar. The more work we put into clearing our mind and preparing it for the new, the better the results we're likely to get. Remember the **frequently asked questions** in Chapter 1? Creativity isn't something which only special people or geniuses can do. It is a capability that we all have, we already use and can develop further. The more we work at it, the easier it will become and the more successful at it we will be.

The Uccello™ Process For Non-Stop Creativity

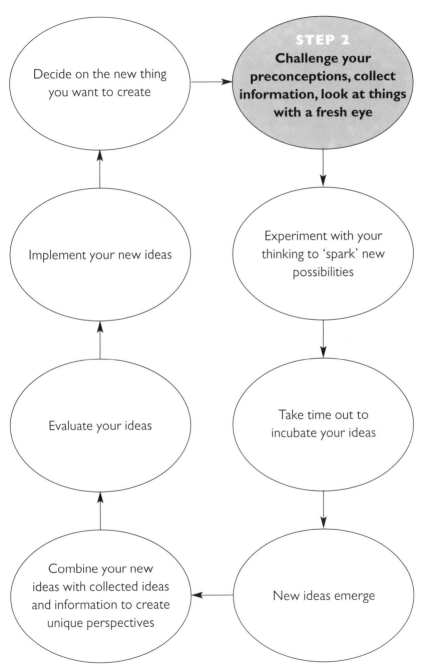

Source: Fiona McLeod and Richard Thomson, 1997.

As you work through this chapter we will help you to identify, experience and practise the behaviours and ways of thinking which will give you the maximum chance of being creative.

Preparing our mind

To prepare your mind you need to look at things with a fresh eye.

In our day-to-day lives we are preoccupied much of the time. We're constantly under pressure and our minds are filled with meeting deadlines, writing reports, shopping for dinner, remembering that birthday. In reality we notice very little. We look but do not really see. This lack of awareness and focus fundamentally affects our ability to be creative.

Hot Tip   *Invite an alien*

In work, to make your meetings more creative invite someone from outside your team, department, division, even organisation to help you see things with a fresh eye and provide new perspectives.

Thinking about how we behave in unfamiliar situations demonstrates how much more aware we can be. For instance, think back to your first day in a new job. How observant were you? The chances are you noticed everything: the layout of the office, the colours, the smells, how tidy or untidy it was, how people were dressed, how they behaved and how you were treated. You were attuned to everything around you. Nothing was familiar and you were constantly looking for clues to help you make sense of the situation. Over time, as days, weeks and months passed, this changed and you became more accustomed to your surroundings; the unfamiliar became the familiar. Now you probably don't see the litter in the car park, you don't notice that the person at reception is preoccupied reading a newspaper or that the office door needs repainting. Your perception has become dulled. If you want insight into how your company operates, ask a new employee. You could be surprised, even shocked at the reply.

Being creative is about seeing possibilities. It's about being attuned to opportunities and making connections other people haven't seen or haven't yet made. To be able to do this means consciously trying to make ourselves receptive to what is going on around us – to what we see, to ideas and to what is happening in the world. If we can open up our mind it will act like radar, both on a conscious and an unconscious level, using our purpose as a focus. It will help us notice things, search for things, pick up ideas and store them away. Our mind works constantly at gathering information which we will select from and combine in a new way.

Looking at things with a fresh eye is about being observant, alert and receptive. It's about being that new employee again! Try this short activity and see how observant you can be.

Activity *3.1 Seeing things afresh*

 This activity takes place in your home. You will need a pen and a notepad or a hand-held tape recorder.

Step 1

If possible, start the activity by briefly going outside of your home. Go for a short walk, go into the garden, go anywhere that takes you out of that space. Spend a few minutes trying to clear your mind and starting to focus.

If you can't or don't want to go outside, choose one room in your home, stand outside it, close the door, clear your mind and start to focus.

Step 2

Walk towards the entrance of your home (or room) and, as you are approaching it, try to imagine that you are seeing it for the first time. You're looking at it as if you were a stranger or an alien from outer space. If it helps, imagine you are putting on a pair of special glasses, which will make you highly observant.

- What does it look like from the outside?
- What kind of door does it have?
- How is that door decorated?
- What other features does it have?
- How well is it maintained?
- Is there anything unusual about it?

▓ Does it suggest anything about the type of person who lives there?

Concentrate on every detail and either write down exactly what you see or record it on your tape recorder.

Step 3
Now go through the door.

▓ What do you see when you enter?
▓ What's your first reaction?
▓ How do you feel?
▓ How is it decorated: the colours, the textures, the style?
▓ What are the paintwork and other surfaces like?
▓ Is there anything broken, damaged? If so, is it recent?
▓ If there is furniture, how is it arranged?
▓ Are there any pictures, objects etc?

Again imagine that you are seeing it for the first time. Look at it through your observation glasses and record in detail exactly what you see.

Step 4
Sit down and relax for several minutes. Now read through your description or listen to it on your tape.

▓ What did consciously concentrating on every detail do to the way you saw your home or your room?
▓ Did you notice anything new?
▓ Was there anything that surprised you?
▓ Was there anything that made you feel uncomfortable?
▓ Did it suggest things you want to do or to change?
▓ Did it suggest any new possibilities?

Seeing things with a fresh eye is about making the familiar, unfamiliar so that we can see things differently, spot opportunities and gain the new perspectives that are so important to being creative.

Practise this technique whenever you can – at work, during a routine journey or, perhaps, simply looking at an object. It is surprising how much it can 'spring clean' our mind and spur us on to creative action.

Chance favours only the prepared mind.   Louis Pasteur

Being observant and alert also opens us to chance events. Originality often springs from serendipitous or chance encounters and many innovations are the result of accidental discoveries.

Hot Tip

 When we're consciously involved in the search for a new idea we adopt these behaviours. We should, however, try to make being observant and seeing things afresh a way of life. By doing so we increase the likelihood of us being consistently creative and of producing original ideas. Clients regularly tell us that adopting these new behaviours changes the way they think and, ultimately their lives.

Here are just a few examples of new ideas that have come about as a result of a chance occurrence.

Pharmacia, a world leader in pharmaceuticals, owes its original success to the chance discovery that a contamination in sugar was an ideal substitute for blood plasma.

The inventor of Velcro, George de Mestral, was out walking with his dog when his trousers became covered with burrs. When he got home he examined them under his microscope and saw the small hooks that made the burrs stick so firmly to the tiny loops of the fabric. At that moment he saw how to make a unique two-sided fastener, one side with stiff hooks like the burrs and the other side with soft loops like the fabric of his trousers.

Post-it Notes were born when Spence Silver, a researcher for 3M, was looking for a stronger adhesive and discovered by chance an odd glue that did not stick permanently. Several years later one of his colleagues, Art Fry, was looking for a temporary bookmark and found that there was none on the market. He remembered Silver's glue and together they developed the idea of Post-it Notes.

Other examples of ideas that have resulted from chance discoveries include: penicillin, offset printing and saccharin.

To get ourselves in the right frame of mind to be creative we can practise what is often called 'being in the flow' or being 'in the moment'. Think about what happens when you're completely involved in an activity. You could be playing a sport, a game, a musical instrument, you could be dancing or doing something else physically demanding such as climbing. How do you feel when you are doing it? You're totally engrossed and all outside distractions disappear. Your awareness of everything is heightened and your whole mind and body are channelled into that experience. You're totally focused on the moment. When you're working creatively this is exactly how it feels and the more you can open yourself up and concentrate on what you're doing the more 'in the flow' you become.

Mihaly Csikszentmihalyi, professor in psychology at the University of Chicago, has spent over twenty years researching, what he calls, this 'optimal experience' and has identified a number of elements which are usually present during it. They are:

- It involves a challenging activity requiring skills.
- Attention is completely absorbed by the activity.
- There are clear goals and immediate feedback.
- The mind clears of irrelevant information.
- There is a sense of being in control.
- There is a loss of self-consciousness.
- Our sense of time bears little relationship to real time.
- The activity is an end in itself and is intrinsically rewarding.
   (Mihaly Csikszentmihalyi, *Flow: The Psychology of Happiness*,
   Rider, 1992)

Csikszentmihalyi's research also shows that there is a strong link between this type of experience and people's level of happiness and well-being. So not only is being creative enjoyable and highly productive, it's also good for you!

When we are running workshops with clients using the Uccello™ Process, during the ideas-generating session there is a period of time where the participants become totally 'in the moment', absorbed and unselfconscious. During this they are at their most creative and, in about an hour, generate more than a hundred fully formed ideas in relation to their chosen business purpose.

This short activity, using your sense of taste as the focus, will help you to begin to experience and practise being 'in the moment'. It also demonstrates how this state of heightened awareness and focus can intensify and change the way we experience things.

Activity *3.2 In the moment*

 You will need two raisins and a quiet, comfortable place to sit.

Step 1
Begin by closing your eyes and relaxing. Scan briefly through your body for any tension. Focus on your legs, then up to your waist, then your chest, back, head and face. Settle down and begin to let go. Be aware of your breathing. Breathe in and out and try to relax more with each outward breath. Repeat this three times.

Step 2
You are now going to spend the next minute concentrating on the experience of eating a raisin. Take the raisin and place it in your mouth. Don't bite it or suck it, just let it sit on your tongue. Feel the texture of the fruit and taste its slight sweetness. Now move the raisin around your mouth. Feel how it softens, how the texture changes and the taste becomes more ripe. Then slowly bite into it and experience the intensity of the taste. Now swallow the raisin.

Step 3
Sit quietly for a few moments. Now take the second raisin and, having relaxed, repeat the exercise, this time making it last for a full minute.

Step 4

Now go back over the experience and reflect on it.

- Did the raisin taste differently when you concentrated on eating it?
- Did you manage to clear your mind of other material?
- How did you feel during the activity?
- Did you lose your sense of time?
- How did you feel once you had finished the activity?

Hot Tip *Using triggers*

In our daily lives we need something to remind ourselves to be observant, alert and 'in the moment'. Something which will act as a trigger. One technique that works well is to take ten self-adhesive coloured dots and stick them in prominent places in your home and at work. Go through your daily routine and select places and objects you go to frequently or use regularly, e.g. your kettle, your mirror, your computer. Each time you see a dot it will act as a trigger and help you pause and step outside of your normal way of thinking.

Challenging our preconceptions

During Step 2 of the Uccello™ Process when we are in the preparation phase, as well as becoming more receptive, we need to challenge our preconceptions, our attitudes and beliefs.

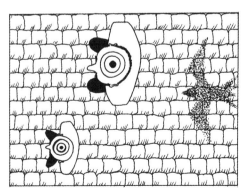

A bird's eye view of the world

In our daily lives we each view things differently. Our eyes receive patterns of stimulation from which we each construct our own world. Our perception is subjective and we fill in and filter out information according to our own view of the world. We process information by matching present events against past experiences. The more vivid the past experience the easier it is to match. These memories shape the way we see and understand the world.

It's this ability to 'recognise' that makes perception so powerful and enables us to function effectively in the world. We can respond to situations instantly even with only limited information. A flashing red light signals danger and we're immediately alert and ready to act. We learn from experience and become more receptive to patterns that remind us of situations we dealt with effectively. In this way we're able to deal with most situations we encounter without having to rethink and relearn them every time.

This process, however, is also limiting. We develop 'mindsets' which means that we become biased in the way we see things. Once we've seen and understood something in a particular way it's extremely difficult to see it differently. We develop blind spots and have difficulty seeing alternative interpretations. We only look where we expect to find something and new information is either ignored or made to fit our worldview. We get locked into ways of seeing things and we assume ours is the right way, the best way and the only way. To be creative it's necessary to question those preconceptions.

Watch the way children behave. They show a freshness, an innocence and an openness, free of any preconceived notions or judgements. There's a willingness to experiment and they're always asking the question 'why?'. They're like learning machines.

Fast Fact

 It was the simple question 'why?' which was the impetus for the invention of the Polaroid camera. Dr Edwin Land's three-year-old daughter was watching him take a photograph and asked 'why can't I see it now?' This innocent question sent Dr Land off on the quest for instant photography.

This naivety is exactly what we, as adults, need to adopt in our personal and working lives to help us recognise and step outside of those mindsets that constrain us.

Creativity and innovation are about finding new perspectives and new ways into information. Simply asking the question 'why?' can help us do that. It's no coincidence that two of our greatest thinkers shared a similar motto.

Einstein's motto was: 'The most important thing is never to stop questioning' and Leonardo da Vinci's was simply: 'I question'.

This short activity demonstrates how firmly we can be locked into our way of thinking and are unaware of our mindsets.

Activity *3.3 Preconceptions and mindsets*

 Step I

Think of a mechanical clock and ask yourself the following questions:

- How many figures does it show on the face?
- How many hands does it have?
- Which way does it go?

Now look at this image of a clock:

Clock designed by Paolo Uccello in 1443 for Florence Cathedral.

How does it differ from our accepted idea of a mechanical clock? First of all it shows 24 hours. Also, it functions according to 'Hora Italica', a way of telling time based on sunrise and sunset used in the middle ages and, perhaps most surprisingly, it goes backwards. If you look back in history clocks functioned in many different ways, but we have become so accustomed to thinking of mechanical clocks going in, what we call a 'clockwise' direction and having only two or three hands, it doesn't occur to us that they could be different.

Here are some other examples of mindsets:

- In 1967 the Swiss invented the quartz movement but because of their tradition and history of excellence in machining, they were blind to the possibilities. In fact they were so confident that it wouldn't catch on that they didn't protect the idea and the new technology was taken up by the Japanese and the Americans. In 1968 Switzerland had 68% of world watch sales and 85% of the profit. Japan had none. Ten years later Japan dominated the market and the Swiss market share had dropped to 10%.
- The QWERTY keyboard is the layout we use for the keyboard in typewriters and computers. Do we use it because it's the most effective way to arrange the keys? Quite the opposite. An engineer named Scholes designed the QWERTY layout specifically to slow typists down. The typewriting machines of the day tended to jam if the typist went too fast. Then, the Remington Sewing Machine Company mass-produced a typewriter using the QWERTY keyboard which meant that lots of typists began to learn the layout. This resulted in other typewriter companies also offering the QWERTY keyboard, and so more typists began to learn it. Now it is the standard used by everyone, even although keyboards no longer have levers that jam and there are designs that would allow typists to work even faster.
- In the IT industry IBM got locked into the idea of the mainframe computer and were left behind when the market moved to minicomputers. Digital, on the other hand, got locked into the minicomputer. In 1977 their founder Ken Olson went on record as saying, 'There is no reason anyone would want a

computer in their home'. A statement he was later to regret. Steven Jobs, who founded Apple Computers, had a strong commitment, however, to making computers accessible to every man, woman and child and went on to develop the personal computer.

- The idea that the earth was the centre of the planetary system. People believed so strongly that the sun went round the earth that the theory lasted for nearly 1,700 years, even when there was overwhelming evidence to disprove it.
- The idea that the earth was flat.

As adults, then, the way we think and behave becomes routinised and this makes us unobservant and uncritical. We get locked into ways of seeing and doing things which limits our ability to be creative. These mindsets happen to us, not only as individuals, but also in our work groups, our organisations and society in general. To be creative our minds need to be as clear and open as possible. This means working hard to recognise our mindsets and step outside of them. We have to try to escape from these automatic responses, habits and routines. Remember if you do what you've always done, you'll get what you've always got!

Every new idea looks crazy at first.   Alfred North Whitehead

During the search for ideas, we become a creator and an inventor. To do this we need to be tolerant of ambiguity and must try to suspend judgement. By that we mean we shouldn't immediately run with our first idea or our first solution to a problem, but should go on generating ideas, keeping the creative tension going as long as we can sustain it. This will give us the best chance of coming up with a truly original idea. Developing ideas is a fragile process and we need to give ourselves sufficient time and space to do it. If we close down the ideas generating process too early we'll stem the flow and stifle our creativity.

Hot Tip   *Be a 'yes and' person*

In work to help produce the best ideas, be a 'yes and' person, not a 'yes but' person. Encourage, support and build on other people's ideas. Don't shoot them down or laugh at them.

Here is your chance to solve a real-life business problem practising suspending judgement.

Activity *3.4 Suspending judgement*

 Step 1
Read the following brief for your business challenge:

> You are employed as a branch manager with one of the major supermarkets. Your branch is in close competition with a neighbouring rival store, and to retain existing customers and attract new ones your company has decided to put on a regular series of promotions on selected goods. These will change weekly.
>
> How can you encourage customers to change their usual shopping pattern and buy more of the promoted items?

Step 2
Take five minutes to generate as many ideas as you can to solve the problem. Write them down as you go along. Remember don't evaluate them, you're looking for quantity, not quality.

Step 3
Keep going for another five minutes. Try to come up with at least another five ideas and capture them. Again, don't filter out your ideas, in fact the crazier they seem, the better!

Step 4
Now take a few moments to think about what happened:

- When you started did you find it easy or difficult to generate ideas?
- Did you find it easier or more difficult the longer you went on?
- At any point did you seem to be stuck?
- Was this block followed by a rush of ideas?

Look at the ideas and choose the one that you think is: (a) the most appropriate solution; (b) the craziest solution.

- Is your most appropriate solution a variation on something you already know?
- Is your crazy idea *really* crazy or just a little different?

Step 5
Turn to page 48 to find the real solution. Did you come up with the same thing or an idea close to it?

When we're generating ideas if we run with our first idea the likelihood is that it will be relatively predictable. If, however, we can suspend judgement and push for more, we'll have a better chance of breaking out of our normal ways of thinking and producing original ideas.

Before going on to the next part of this chapter, *Building blocks for new ideas*, we would like you to try something.

Read this short extract from *Alice's Adventures in Wonderland* by Lewis Carroll. It describes the beginning of Alice's adventures just after she has seen the White Rabbit. Using what you have learned in this chapter, see if you can spot aspects of her behaviour that would help you be more creative.

There was nothing so very remarkable in that; nor did Alice think it so very much out of the way to hear the Rabbit say to itself. 'Oh dear! Oh dear! I shall be late!' (when she thought it over afterwards, it occurred to her that she ought to have wondered at this, but at the time it all seemed quite natural); but when the Rabbit actually took a watch out of its waistcoat-pocket, and looked at it, and then hurried on, Alice started to her feet, for it flashed across her mind that she had never before seen a Rabbit with either a waistcoat-pocket, or a watch to take out of it, and burning with curiosity, she ran across the field after it, and was just in time to see it pop down a large rabbit-hole under the hedge.
(From *Alice's Adventures in Wonderland* by Lewis Carroll, Macmillan, 1865)

How many of these did you get?

- Observant
- Relaxed
- Able to see possibilities
- Fearless

▓ Willing to take risks
▓ Curious.

These are the characteristics of the creative person. The more we can make them a way of life, the closer we will be to producing our winning ideas.

Building blocks for new ideas

If you have worked through the activities in the previous section, you will be well on your way to being ready for creativity. Your mind will be clear, open and receptive. It will be focused on your purpose and poised for action. So what else do you have to do to prepare your mind?

Think back to our definition of creativity – bringing together ideas, elements and information to form something new. To stimulate and fuel this process, as well as opening up our mind and giving ourselves the blank canvas to work on, we have to provide it with the materials to work with. This means making sure it has an extensive and varied mix of ingredients that it can use to make those unique combinations. The better the raw material it has at its disposal, the better quality the end result will be. Imagine your mind as a bank – the more you deposit, the more you'll be able to draw out. If, however, you don't put anything in, as in real life, you can't expect to get anything out.

To create this rich store we have to become 'information addicts'. We need to develop a hunger for information, seeking it out whenever and wherever possible. And by 'information' we don't simply mean facts, data or printed material, although these are crucial sources, but also ideas, observations, experiences and knowledge – anything that will broaden our horizons, stimulate new ways of looking at things and help spark off new combinations. Like Alice we need to become curiouser and curiouser.

But this is not information gathering for its own sake. It has a purpose; it's almost as if we're looking for the key that will unlock the door to our new idea. We're on a quest. We know what our destination is: *I want a new . . .* but we don't quite know how to get there. Using our purpose as antennae, we're travelling through the world of information and experience discovering the route as we go. Along the way we're searching for clues and signposts that will point us in the right direction. There may be dead ends, there may be detours, but ultimately our curiosity and sense of purpose will take us to our chosen destination.

If you look at people who consistently come up with new business ideas, they are information oriented. They possess a deep curiosity and fascination, but it is always shaped and directed by their desire to identify that new opportunity, to see round the corner and to make that connection which no one else has made. As they trawl the world of information and experience, they're searching for that insight which could give them the way into their new idea and allow that unique combination to happen.

So we need to make sure that our brain has the stimulation it needs to make these new and unusual connections. But there's another important aspect: the more diverse and unrelated the elements we combine, the more the potential for uniqueness. Take a moment to think about it. If we put together 'obvious', related things, what is the outcome likely to be? The chances are that other people will have already seen and made that connection, so the potential for originality is limited. If, however, we're prepared to push it further, work at it harder by combining disparate and unconnected items, we'll be rewarded with a greater degree of uniqueness. Try Activity 3.5 to see how this works.

Activity *3.5 Escaping the obvious*

 Step 1
Remember Activity 1.1, when you invented a brand new game by combining a newspaper, a fish, a clock and a hat. We would like you to do the same again, come up with an idea for a new game, but this time the items we want you to use are: a *bat*, a *ball*, a *watch* and a *notepad*.

Take five minutes to generate as many ideas as you can for a new game using only those four items. Record them on a pad or a flipchart.

Step 2
Now look at your ideas.

- Do they resemble games that already exist?
- Do they use the items in a straightforward way?
- On a scale of 1–10 how unusual are the games?

Now compare them with the ideas that you generated in Activity 1.1. On the same scale, rate those ideas.

The likelihood is that the games that you came up with in Activity 3.5 will resemble games that you know and have played. Combining the elements may have felt easier but the end result is likely to be less imaginative or inventive. The more unusual, the more diverse the elements you use in combining, the more original your new idea is likely to be. It's like suspending judgement, the longer we can keep the creative tension going and the more we wrestle consciously and unconsciously with the process, the greater the chances for originality. It may be harder work but it will help us to escape the obvious.

Our mind needs stimulation if it is to come up with new and imaginative ideas. Are you giving your brain the stimulation it needs? Think about the area you work in. What do you have on your desk, other than your telephone and possibly your computer? A photograph? A calendar? Anything else? What's on the walls? A wall chart? Maybe there's a picture? How stimulating is this environment? If you were to visit an artist's studio the scene is likely to be very different. The walls would probably be covered in a mass of images: postcards, sketches, drawings, magazine cuttings, pictures from books and scraps of paper. There would be a whole array of objects: things gathered from nature, bits of junk and a range of artefacts collected over time. All this provides a rich source of stimulation to fuel the creative process. We're back to the idea of bringing together as diverse a range of elements as possible. Creativity is essentially an 'eclectic' process and the more eclectic we can become, the greater the potential for truly creative ideas.

Fast Fact

 Edwin Land, the founder of Polaroid, kept a garden atrium at the organisation's headquarters and encouraged his people to tend it during office hours. By doing this not only was he trying to stimulate creativity, but he was making a very definite statement about the desirability and legitimacy of creativity within the organisation.

Now clearly we're not suggesting that you turn your office into an artist's studio, but what could you do to make the environment more stimulating? Do you have a pin-board that could be used? Is there an area in the office that you could make more conducive to creativity? Take a few minutes to consider what changes you could make to your work environment.

If you don't give your mind the stimulation it needs you are putting it at a serious disadvantage. Your mind is working constantly, both on a conscious and an unconscious level (see Chapter 5), sifting through, sorting out and synthesising information. Make sure it has the right stuff to work with!

Activity 3.6 New experiences

 We'd like you to identify and list 10 different activities that you could do, in your personal and professional life, to stimulate your thinking and gather diverse information. And remember, information isn't just facts, data etc., it's also ideas and experiences, in fact anything that will help you to see things differently and enrich the raw material that your mind has to work with.

Once you have done this, turn to the end of the chapter and compare your list with our suggestions. If, every day, you can do at least one thing from either of these lists, as well as enhancing your life experience, it will provide you with the building blocks you will need to be highly creative.

Fast Fact

 Sir Basil Spence, the architect of Coventry Cathedral, was flicking through a natural history magazine when he came across an enlargement of the eye of a fly and this gave him the idea for the vault of the cathedral.

In the creative process, then, everything is a potential source of ideas. Travel, reading, films, TV, visiting galleries and museums, listening to music, talking to people who have different outlooks and viewpoints to our own and, of course, looking at nature – all these will help to fuel creative thinking.

This search for information also presents us with an ideal opportunity to break out of our normal routines and challenge our preconceptions and mindsets. Do you always read the same newspapers and the same magazines? If so, break the habit and read something different. If you usually read a broadsheet, try a tabloid. Buy an unusual magazine you normally wouldn't consider. You don't have to read it all, just skim through it and see if anything jumps out at you. Similarly, do you only watch certain types of TV programmes? If you never watch wildlife programmes or costume dramas, try watching a bit of one; you might find that your opinion of them in the past has been a mindset. Also, in our day-to-day lives we tend to stick with people who share our worldview, so next time you're travelling or at an event, make a point of talking to someone new. Listen to them and see what you can learn. Search out those new experiences and do things you've never done before. As we've said, creativity is an eclectic process and the more varied and diverse the activities you're involved in, the richer and more original the results will be.

In workshops we suggest that people go out and buy magazines and periodicals that have nothing to do with their work or hobbies and that are completely out of the ordinary for them. Recently a participant, who worked for a major finance company, related how he'd gone home and read his wife's copy of *Nursing Times*. In it was an article on an HR initiative going on in the Health Service which he had been able to modify and apply in his own job.

When you're involved in your search, remember that information about change is particularly important because change creates opportunity. If you're looking for that competitive idea, the one that's going to make you stand out from the crowd, don't spend time analysing the past, but look to the future. There are already signs of what it will look like and if you can spot them, then there's a good chance that you can produce that winning idea. Look at what's happening in the world. How are lifestyles changing? What are the trends and demographic changes? Watch what young people are doing. Talk to them, find out what they think and how they see the world. Look for what's new in the marketplace. What are companies doing? Where are they going? And don't just follow what's happening in your own industry or field, but watch other industries and occupations. Then ask yourself whether there is anything there for you? Is there anything that you could use, that you could combine with something else to make a unique idea? This information and your own perceptiveness will help you to see opportunities and ideas that are not easily apparent. You'll be able to spot the gaps and make the connections that no one else has yet made.

Now you're going to begin the process of building up a rich bank of information that will help you generate your new idea.

Activity *3.7 Looking to the future*

 We would like you to spend some time thinking about what is happening at the moment in various areas. You'll be using this information in Chapter 6 in the combining process, so please record and keep it.

Step 1

Firstly, we would like you to identify ten new things that are happening within your work group or organisation. If you are self-employed or are considering going into business, think about what new things your peers or people you know are doing or new things they're involved in.

Step 2

Now identify ten new things that are happening in your industry or your field of work. Again, if you are thinking about going into business, you might have a broad idea of the sort of area you would like to work in. Think about any new developments that are going on there and list them.

Step 3

Now identify ten new things that are happening in other industries and in other fields. Look for things that are pushing the boundaries, that are at the cutting edge of work and business.

Step 4

Now identify ten new things that are happening in the world in general. These could come from the news, they could be about trends, demographic changes, anything that will help you to tap into the future.

Once you've done this take a few minutes to read over what you've written, familiarise yourself with it, then put your list aside for use in Chapter 6. You've now given your mind some high voltage material to work with and it will have already begun consciously and unconsciously to process it and make new connections.

Magpie thinking

Lastly, in your quest for a winning idea you might practise what we call 'magpie thinking' – stealing ideas and pieces of information and incorporating them into a new idea. Fred Smith, the founder of Fedex, foresaw the need for efficient, instant delivery of information and borrowed the principle of centralised distribution from the banking industry as a model for his company's operation.

If you look at advertising and art, for decades they have consistently stolen images from one another. Many famous ads have been based on or featured well-known paintings and sculptures, while numerous artists have freely used the subject matter of advertising in their work.

You've now completed the preparation stage of the Uccello™ Process and you should be in an ideal frame of mind to come up with that winning idea. In Chapter 4, you're going to consciously play with your thinking to explore your purpose, to find new ways of looking at it and to spark off new creative possibilities.

Solution to Activity 3.4

The store manager arranged that, in the aisles where the promoted items were on display, the climate was subtly different. On hot days the air was cooler, on cool days it was warmer. In these aisles they also used faint but noticeable fragrances such as spring flowers and newly baked bread to encourage customers to linger and so buy more.

Suggestions for Activity 3.6

Travel   One of the best ways of expanding our worldview and helping us to see things differently is through travel. It takes us out of our normal environment and routine and we are exposed to different cultures, experiences and challenges. Also, when we return home, we see our own surroundings anew. Travel can help us recognise and break down those powerful mindsets.

Films and TV   Films and television are a rich source of ideas and learning. Not only can they provide new information, but often the subject matter and the way the director or producer handles it can help us gain important insights into future trends and 'hot' topics.

Conversations   As well as being an important source of information, speaking to new people will also help you to gain different perspectives and broaden your worldview. Next time you're travelling or at an event, either social or work related, make a point of talking to someone you don't know. Similarly at work, when you're at the coffee machine or having lunch, sit next to someone from a different department or division and engage them in conversation. The cross-fertilisation of ideas and information could provide the stimulus for a new idea.

Music Listening to music can be one of the most stimulating and satisfying activities we can engage in. Not only will it fuel your imagination, but, if you try listening to different types of music, it can open whole new areas of experience.

Nature The natural world is one of the best – some would say *the* best – sources of ideas and inspiration. Numerous inventions and new ideas have come about from looking at nature and how it works and applying the principles to the man-made world. The idea for the ring-pull can, for example, came from looking at the way we peel a banana.

Reading Reading both fiction and non-fiction provides us with a wealth of material to use in the creative process. Here, as with information gathering as a whole, eclecticism is the key. Anything could spark off that new idea, that new combination. Many famous business leaders are avid readers, dipping into subjects as diverse as philosophy, drama, history, even poker!

Hobbies Take up a new hobby. This will open up your mind to new information and help to change your existing ways of seeing and thinking about things.

Internet This provides a vast repository of information that is being added to hourly. Dip into it to answer questions or simply search for random words and phrases to discover fascinating new facts and information.

4
Experiment With Your Thinking

Step 3 of the Uccello™ Process

You have now arrived at Step 3 of the Uccello™ Process where you will experiment with your thinking. At Step 2 you worked at getting yourself into the right frame of mind to be creative and now you're going to start on that blank canvas you've created, pushing your thinking and escaping the confines that normally constrain it. You will be taking your purpose statement and consciously playing with it to help spark off new ideas and creative possibilities. Before doing that, however, let's take a few minutes to think a bit more about the process of being creative.

Why do you think it is so difficult to come up with a new idea or a new way of doing something? If you've worked through the book so far you might have answered that it's because of our mindsets or because we get locked into things. If you did, then, well done. That's exactly what does happen and much of Chapter 3 was about the importance of recognising these mindsets and working to overcome them. But there is something else at work that makes it difficult to generate truly new ideas. The reason we get locked into ways of seeing and doing things isn't just because we get mentally lazy, although as we've seen we do fall into routines, but it also has to do with the way the brain works.

In our daily lives our senses are bombarded by huge amounts of information that the brain has to process if we are to make sense of the world and be able to respond to it. The brain consists of a vast network of interconnecting pathways that carry the information we receive from the senses to areas where it is then processed and passed on. Imagine the brain as a sophisticated telephone exchange. At any one time it receives innumerable individual calls that it computes and organises, connecting each caller to the right

The Uccello™ Process For Non-Stop Creativity

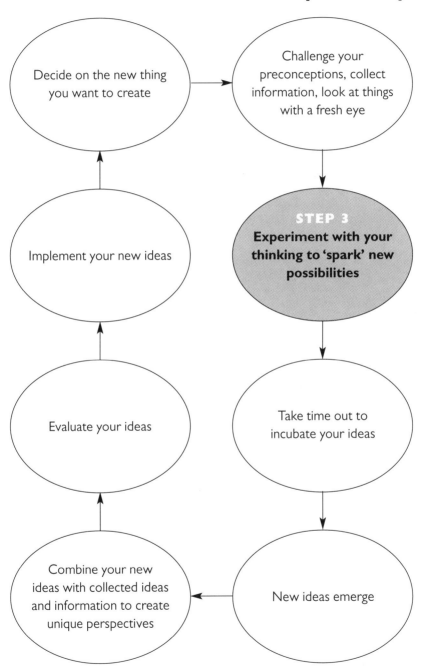

Source: Fiona McLeod and Richard Thomson, 1997.

receiver. The first time a call comes in the exchange doesn't know who the sender is or where to send it, so it will take some time to find and connect the call to the correct receiver. In the future, however, if it receives the same incoming signal the exchange begins to recognise the sender and remembers where to send it. Over time, if it has to deal with the same sender repeatedly, this connection becomes a permanent stored path that is automatically triggered connecting the sender to the receiver. With repetition, this process will become faster and more efficient.

And that is exactly how we make sense of the world. We build up a network of stored pathways in our brains and we use these to interpret what happens to us. For example, as children we learn by being shown an object and hearing the corresponding word being sounded. We are shown an apple and our parent or teacher says the word, 'apple'. With repetition, when we hear the word, 'apple' we will automatically visualise an apple or when we see the fruit itself we associate it with the sound of the word 'apple'. In this way our brains form a connection between the two. But we also touch the apple and when we handle it we feel the smoothness of the skin and so a path is formed between the word 'apple', the sight of an apple and the idea of smoothness. Other connections will be made with taste, smell and so on and the sum total of all these memory traces will make up our idea of an apple. So when we experience any of these sensations it connects with and triggers off the idea of an apple that is stored in our mind.

In this way we are interpreting the world in terms of past experience and of what we already know. Once these pathways, these memory traces have been established, they are extremely useful because they enable us to process large amounts of information very quickly and efficiently and to respond to them. This is what makes perception such an incredibly powerful tool.

But there is a price to be paid for this efficiency. This matching process that sends the information down the established pathways and connects it to existing memory traces means that we'll interpret everything in relation to what already exists in our brain. New information we receive will be added to that which already exists and the new 'memory' that is formed will be the basis on which we'll interpret incoming information in the future. This process makes it extremely difficult to see things differently and to make the unusual connections so essential for generating new ideas.

To be creative we need to break out of the confines that this processing mechanism imposes on us. To make those new connections and produce those new and winning ideas we need to force our mind, almost trick it out of these existing pathways. This means finding new ways of looking at and processing the information that our senses take in so that we can find new and different perspectives.

For this reason we need to experiment with our thinking, we need to play with it consciously, actively sending information down different pathways so that we can find new ways into it and so make different connections. Experimenting helps us loosen these restrictions and break out of the confines of our usual, set way of thinking. That is why it is often called 'thinking out of the box'.

Let's try something to set the scene for experimenting. Think of a board measuring 24" × 24" comprising alternate black and white squares. What comes to mind? The chances are you associated it with playing a game and maybe thought of various games that you know. Now imagine a set of draughts or chequers on the board, what does that do to how you see it? It immediately changes how you think about the board. The likelihood is that you now see it as a series of straight lines and diagonals with pieces only being able to move over the board in these prescribed lines. If the board is now set up for a game of chess how does that alter the way in which you think of it? The rules of the game change and now you might see it as being made up of diagonals, straight lines and L-shapes for

Knight moves. But imagine if you took away the pieces altogether. What else could you use the board for? It could be a tabletop, a place mat, something to put a vase on or it could be hung on the wall as a minimalist work of art!

It is the automatic connections that we make between things and the 'rules' we apply that determine how we think about something and what we think we can or cannot do with it. As long as these connections are undisturbed and the 'rules' stay in place, it is very difficult to think differently. But if we consciously experiment and, for instance, we substitute chess pieces for chequers, if we add something or take everything away, we can push the information down different pathways and that will lead us to new ideas.

Humour works in a very similar way to the creative process. Here are some simple jokes. You may not find them funny, but if you do, what is it that makes them so?

- Have you put the cat out? I didn't know it was on fire.
- A man came to the door in his pyjamas. What's a door doing in his pyjamas?
- A man walks into a bar. He says, 'Ouch'. It was an iron bar.

So what does happen when somebody tells you a joke? Obviously if it is funny the end result will be that you laugh, but think about what leads up to that. It starts with the person who is telling the joke saying something; they could pose a question, make a statement or tell a little story. Whichever it is, they are giving you information that you will immediately begin to organise and try to make sense of. The person is setting up an expectation, a tension about what's going to happen and where the story is going. Then they deliver the punch line and it forces you to reconsider completely what they told you initially. Two conflicting pieces of information are brought together and as result, your expectations are turned on their head and you get a completely new perspective on the original infor-mation. The point at which that happens and you get the joke is very like the 'aha' moment, the moment when you have a new idea.

In this way jokes disrupt our pre-programmed connections. They push incoming information out of their normal pathways and into new ones. They force us to see things differently.

This is exactly the purpose of experimenting in Step 3 of the Uccello™ Process. Here we are consciously using triggers and techniques to play with our thinking to try to break out of those pre-programmed pathways and connections that restrict the way we think and limit our ability to be creative.

There is a whole range of techniques that can be used here, some of which you might have already come across. Synectics, originally developed by W. J. J. Gordon, brainstorming, devised by Alex Osborne, and the many lateral thinking techniques pioneered by Edward de Bono are all powerful tools for experimenting with your thinking. Here we are going to work with five techniques: 'Re-defining', 'Opposites', 'What's not there', 'Random input' and 'Metaphor'. When running workshops we find that these provide people with a good range, some that focus more on language, for instance, 'Re-defining', and others that work with images and pictures such as 'Metaphor'.

Now you're going to take your purpose statement and apply these different techniques to it.

Activity *4.1 Re-defining your purpose*

 Look back to Activity 3.4, Suspending judgement, on page 39 where you came up with an idea for how to encourage customers to buy promoted items. What do you think your purpose statement would have been? Perhaps, 'I want a new way to sell promoted items'. How else could you define that? You could possibly say, 'I want a new way to reward customers who buy promoted products'. Or another way might be, 'I want a new way to discourage customers from buying these promoted items from our competitors'. In each of these statements we're looking at the purpose from a different angle and each one of these points us in a different direction for possible ideas. The first statement focuses on selling the items, so you might have someone talking to customers, offering them free samples etc. The second statement suggests rewarding people in some way so you could have a prize for the person who spends the most on promoted items in a week or a 'best shopper' award for the person who, over a month, changes most often from their usual brand to the promoted item. Statement three, however, focuses on making the competition a less attractive option, so you could rent a crowd to slow down shoppers at their checkouts!

Just doing something as simple as re-defining our purpose creates new perspectives and sparks off new ideas. Now try re-defining your own purpose statement.

Step 1

First of all we would like you to take your purpose statement and spend five minutes coming up with as many ideas as you can to meet it. Record these on a flip-chart or a piece of paper.

Step 2

Now write down four re-definitions of your purpose statement.

Step 3

Take each of these definitions in turn and come up with some ideas to meet each of them. Take about 10–15 minutes to do this.

Step 4

Look at all the ideas that you have generated and ask yourself the following questions:

- To what extent were the ideas that you came up with at Step 3 more unusual than those at Step 1?
- Why do you think they are different?
- Are there any that surprise you? If so why?
- What did re-defining do to the way you thought about your purpose?

Step 5

Now select two ideas that you particularly like and jot them down. You will be using them to combine at Step 6 of the process.

'Re-defining' is a useful technique for finding different ways of looking at our purpose and producing unusual ideas. Now we're going to look at 'What's not there', which helps us to focus outside of the information we normally work with and escape the tried and tested routes we tend to go down.

4.2 What's not there

 This is one of our favourite techniques and a very simple one to use. It involves taking your purpose and asking yourself 'what's not there?' currently in relation to it.

Here are some examples of 'What's not there' in action:

- In the 1980s a major food company was looking for a way to increase sales of its best-selling product. They had come to dominate the market and their sales of the product had plateaued. If they were to produce a purpose statement it might have been, 'We want a new way to increase sales of our product'. The company looked at what was currently not there in terms of sales and came up with the idea of competitors, i.e. they were not selling to them. So they then decided to sell the raw ingredients for making their product to their competitors who could produce their own brand using these ingredients. As a result of this the company managed to create a virtual monopoly on the market by selling their own brand as well as raw ingredients to their competitors.
- When Black and Decker were looking for a new product they looked at all the power tools that they had developed and asked themselves 'what's not there?'. The answer was a table on which to use the tools and the result was the 'Workmate'.
- In a recent workshop one of our clients was working on new ways of advertising their company. Their purpose statement was, 'We want to find a new way to communicate our voice to the world'. They asked themselves what was currently not there in relation to that, and amongst other things, they came up with the idea of humour. They then went on to produce a very witty and successful series of ads using cartoons to communicate their message.

Now try applying this technique to your own purpose.

Step 1
Take your purpose and ask yourself what currently is not there in relation to it. Take 5–10 minutes to jot down as many ideas as you can.

Step 2
Now look at your ideas:

- Are there any that surprise you? If so, why?
- If you've already done any of the other experimenting activities in what way are these ideas different?
- Why do you think this is?
- What did looking outside the information do to your thinking?

Step 3
Now select two ideas that you particularly like and jot them down. You will be working with them at Step 6 of the Process when you combine your ideas with other information to generate unique ideas.

When we are intensely involved in trying to find a new idea for something or solving a problem we become completely focused on the information that we already have. We forget to look outside of it and this is one of the reasons we tend to come up with variations on ideas that we've already had and find it difficult to generate a new and original idea or solution. Our next technique, 'Opposites', also helps us to frame our purpose differently.

Activity *4.3 Opposites*

 This technique involves taking our purpose statement and looking at the opposite of it. An example of how successfully this can work is 3M's Post-it Notes. At one time their stated goal was: 'To invent adhesives that stick better than those of our competitors'. When Art Fry wanted a temporary bookmark, however, he remembered the weak glue his colleague had produced some time before and so the ubiquitous Post-it Note was born. You could say that instead of producing an adhesive that was stronger than their competitors, they did the opposite.

Step 1

Take your purpose statement and write down the opposite of it. For example, if your purpose was: 'I want a new way to light this room', the opposite would be: 'I want a new way to darken this room'. This might suggest ideas such as removing the windows, using solid shades on all the lights, painting the ceiling black etc.

Step 2

Now spend 15 minutes generating as many ideas as possible to meet your new purpose statement.

Step 3

Take a few minutes to look at your ideas and to think about the process that you have just used.

- How has looking at the opposite of your purpose changed the way you think about it?
- Did it produce any surprises? If so, what?
- If you have done any of the other activities, in what way were these ideas different?

Step 4

Now choose two of your ideas and add them to your list for use in Chapter 6.

Considering the opposite of our purpose changes the focus of our ideas generating process and stands our thinking on its head. It acts as a trigger to help us break out of those established pathways and escape those variations on existing ideas that we tend to come up with. In the next activity, 'Random input', you are going to introduce new information to consciously set up new connections and help spark more original ideas.

Activity *4.4 Random input*

 This technique, developed by Edward de Bono, involves introducing a random word or an unrelated idea into the ideas generating process in order to spark off new creative possibilities or to escape creative S.O.S.

Creative S.O.S.*

Creative S.O.S. stands for creative State of Stuckness. We all know what it is like when we are desperately trying to find a new idea and we get stuck. It's like hitting a brick wall. In this situation try using one of the experimentation techniques or try some incubating (see Chapter 5). If you are already using one of the techniques switch to a different one and see what happens.

Here is an example. One of our clients was concerned about the level of staff turnover in their business and was using the Uccello™ Process to generate ideas for how to reduce it. The purpose they had come up with was: 'We want a new way to retain staff' and they were working through various techniques to explore their thinking. At one point they had reached creative S.O.S. when out of the blue someone said the word 'silk'. The group then went on to explore associations from 'silk' and came up with material, parachute, risk, and skydiving. They went on to develop this further and said why don't we encourage people to leave their comfort zones and stretch themselves both in their personal and professional lives. They then came up with the idea of 'Take a Risk Day' where people could, in a safe environment, try out something developmental which they had always wanted to do but hadn't had the confidence or the opportunity to try it out. The company went on and implemented the idea and it proved very successful. By providing a forum for both personal and professional development and, at the same time, introducing a strong element of fun into the workplace, they improved motivation and created a greater sense of belonging, which resulted in people wanting to stay with the company longer.

Fast Fact

'Random input' is used by many people both in business and in the arts to escape S.O.S. and fuel the creative process. When working in the recording studio, the artist, musician and record producer Brian Eno has a set of cards on which are printed a series of statements which he introduces randomly throughout the recording process to stimulate new approaches and force new connections and combinations.

Now you are going to use 'Random input' to force new connections and combinations in relation to your purpose.

Step 1
Begin by flicking through a dictionary or thesaurus and pick 20 words at random. Write down each word on a separate piece of paper, fold each piece and place it in a container.

Step 2
Now go back to your purpose statement and begin generating as many ideas as you can to meet it.

Step 3
After five minutes pick out one of the words you prepared earlier and write down four associations from it.

Step 4
Bring your purpose statement and these associations together and see what ideas this sparks off.

Step 5
Work for a further 10–15 minutes using words picked at random from the container.

Step 6
Now look at your ideas and consider the following questions:

- What did introducing random words do to your thinking?
- To what extent did it help you produce less predictable ideas?
- Are you surprised by any of the ideas?
- If so, why?
- To what extent did it help you escape S.O.S.?

Step 7
Select two ideas that you like and add them to your list for use at Step 6 of the Process.

A bunch of bananas*

In workshops we use a version of the 'Random input' technique called 'a bunch of bananas'. When groups are generating ideas we nominate one person from each group to be 'a bunch of bananas person' (by quite literally giving them a bunch of bananas!) and it is their job to help their group think unconventionally and escape creative blocks. When they get stuck or run out of ideas the person throws in a 'banana', i.e. introduces a random word or unrelated idea to take people's thinking down a different pathway and force them to make new connections and combinations.

*Creative S.O.S. and 'a bunch of bananas' have been developed from ideas contained in *Creativity and Problem Solving at Work* by Tudor Rickards, Tower, 1997.

Now we are going to go on and work with 'Metaphor', which is one of the most powerful of the techniques.

 4.5 Using metaphor

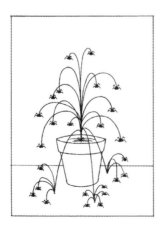

'Metaphor' involves applying an imaginative rather than a literal description to something so that we can look at and explore it in a different way. It's about experiencing and understanding something in terms of something else. For example, if we were looking for a metaphor for an organisation we might say it was a spider plant.

We could then go on to explore this metaphor and the associations that come from it. We could say that the spider plant has a main body with lots of small offshoots. The main plant could be the organisation's head office and the offshoots its departments or divisions. These small offshoots are connected to, and feed off, the main body, so although they are independent they need the main plant for survival. Then we could say that if the main plant isn't kept healthy, fed and watered it will be unable to pass nourishment down to the small offshoots and they will die off. Also, each of these small offshoots is capable of producing new plants and that will ensure that the plant as a whole continues to grow and flourish. Do you see what we're doing? When we use metaphor it helps us to explore our purpose and see it differently.

Here is an example from one of our workshops. Our client was a construction company and the purpose they were working with was, 'We want a new way to create the construction site of the future'. The metaphor which one of the groups came up with was 'a dinner party' and they took us through the associations they had explored. First of all you hold a dinner party for people that are important to you; that was their internal and external customers. Then there is the meticulous planning of the dinner party, you have to make sure you have the right mix of people to make it work; that was about recruitment. There is coming up with a really special menu and making sure that you create the proper ambience; that related to the creative design of the site. Then you have to find the best ingredients; that was to do with the quality of materials on site. And lastly, there is the actual execution of the dinner party with every detail being carried out to perfection; that was to do with the actual day-to-day running of the site. The image that they painted was so vivid and evocative it completely transformed their own and our vision of the construction site of the future. The company have gone on to success-fully implement many of the groundbreaking ideas which came from that workshop.

William Coyne, former vice president of 3M, the company with probably the best and longest track record in creativity and innovation, used the metaphor of a technological nomad to describe 3M. A nomad is someone who wanders the land; in their case the land is the terrain of technology and knowledge. They don't settle down or cling to comfortable or well-known locations and they commit themselves to a lifetime of constant searching. They epitomise what James Dyson has referred to as 'the restless company'.

Now you are going to go on and do the same with your purpose.

Step 1

Take 10 minutes or so to think about your purpose and come up with a metaphor for it. Don't immediately choose the first one that you think of, but consider several options and then select your favourite.

Step 2

Now explore the associations that your metaphor suggests and use these to explore your purpose. Record this on paper. If you want to draw it so much the better! Spend about 20 minutes doing this.

Step 3

Take a few moments to think about your metaphor and its associations.

- How did using a metaphor help you to explore your purpose?
- Which associations in particular sparked off new ways of looking at it?
- How has the experience altered your original vision for your purpose?

Hot Tip

If you draw the metaphor it is a good idea to keep the drawing. Not only will it act as a memory aid for yourself, but it can also provide a very powerful and effective way of communicating your vision to other people.

The brain is a very powerful and sophisticated system capable of processing and transmitting potentially unlimited amounts of information. In our day-to-day lives, however, we only use a fraction of its capacity. If you have worked through this chapter you will have gained some understanding of how it works and have begun to change the patterns of your thinking. As you work through the remaining steps of the Uccello™ Process you will be able to harness even more of its power and push your creativity further, generating those new and winning ideas.

5
Incubate Your Ideas

Step 4 of the Uccello™ Process

In Chapter 2 we talked about how we often wake up in the morning with an idea for how to tackle something that's been bothering us, or we have a new, bright idea for something we would like to do. These ideas don't appear by magic. They're the result of our unconscious mind working on something and, while in a state of deep relaxation, we make connections that we probably wouldn't have made while conscious. When we're active and fully alert our thinking tends to be constrained by our existing mindsets and preconceptions and this reduces the chances of us producing a truly novel idea.

Unfortunately, many people think that this is the only way to come up with a creative idea; that having puzzled about something while they were awake and failed to find a solution, they have to wait until one appears. Luckily for those seeking solutions to problems this often does happen, but unluckily, this compounds their belief that this is the best way for them to access creative ideas. Incubation has long been recognised as a necessary part of generating ideas and it would be wrong to ignore it. It would be equally wrong, however, to depend on it as the *only* way to do it.

The unconscious is a wonderful aid to helping us break out of the strictures we impose on ourselves. When we are conscious we're bound by our own set of rules about what we can and cannot do; we can't help thinking about whether an idea is practical and can be implemented. We constantly evaluate and limit our ideas by not making connections with other things because we consider them not to be relevant to our needs. Thank goodness then for our unconscious mind that ignores all these self-imposed limitations.

What we're suggesting is that to generate truly creative ideas we must actively engage both our conscious and our unconscious

The Uccello™ Process For Non-Stop Creativity

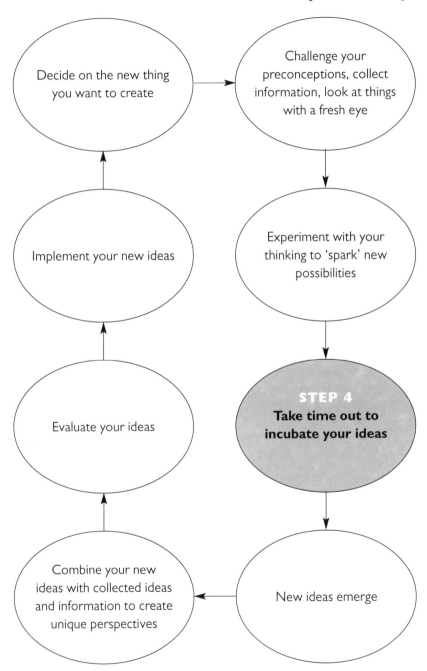

Source: Fiona McLeod and Richard Thomson, 1997.

mind. By doing this we can take control of our creativity and can generate ideas whenever and wherever we want.

Capturing ideas

Try to get into the habit of keeping a notepad and pen with you at all times. You never know when you're going to get a new idea. Make sure you have them by your bedside so that if you awake during the night with an idea, you can capture it quickly. If you don't, you are most likely to lose it and you won't remember it in the morning.

When we awake with a new idea it is usually in connection with something we've been considering or puzzling over. The fact that we have been dwelling on something that we want to create or that's not how we want it to be, is the driver that sets up the tension needed for the creative process to begin and is what causes ideas to come into our minds while we sleep. In the first step of the Uccello™ Process when we decide what it is we want to generate ideas about, we are setting up a similar tension. When we're being creative we need to have a purpose, something that acts as the driver for our ideas generation. Then we have to prepare our mind by consciously challenging our preconceptions and mindsets and giving it the raw material it will need to generate new ideas. We then go on and experiment with our thinking, exploring our purpose in many different ways. By this time we may have at least one idea, possibly more, for the new thing that we want to create. If, at this point we enlist the help of our unconscious, we increase the likelihood of generating many more unusual or radical ideas.

However, this does not mean that we have to go to sleep, although that would be very effective. To enlist our unconscious in making unusual connections we simply need to find ways to slow our brainwaves down from their waking rate of between 13 and 40 cycles per second to around 8 to 12 cycles per second or slower.

For a long time scientists have known that the electrical activity of the brain could be measured and they identified four categories of brainwaves: Alpha, Beta, Theta and Delta.

Beta waves are the fastest and are an indication of an actively engaged mind; we spend most of our waking time in this state. When we're asleep our brainwaves are pulsating at their slowest and we are in a Delta state. When we're relaxing, perhaps we've been busy and we sit down to rest or we take a stroll in the park during our lunch break, we're likely to be in an Alpha state. When we daydream or we're doing something very repetitive that requires little or no active thought we might move into a Theta state. We are also in a Theta state just before we fall asleep and just before we awake. The motorist who spends a lot of time driving on long motorway journeys will often find himself in a Theta state; the runner, the swimmer or rock climber who finds herself 'in the moment' is in a Theta state; this is also the state we're often in when taking a bath or a shower. It's at those times when we have those 'Eureka' moments of inspiration. In this state we are able to make unusual connections and come up with new and novel ideas. That's why so many people will tell you that they have their best ideas in the shower or in the car on their way home.

Hot Tip   *'Time out'*

 Think about all the things you could do to take 'time out' to incubate. When you're generating ideas and you need to incubate them, pick your favourite way of getting into a Theta state and take time out to do it.

Think how easy it is to daydream when you are doing something repetitive – mowing the lawn, pressing your clothes, tidying your desk, cleaning the house, anything that allows you to get into that quiet state when you're not thinking about anything in particular. So we don't have to 'sleep on it', we can create the same effect by doing something different that allows us to slow our brainwaves down.

The following activity is one way of relaxing into a Theta state.

Activity   *5.1 Relaxation*

 When you first do this exercise we suggest reading the following instructions into a portable tape recorder then you will be able to play them back to yourself. Once you have done the exercise a few times you probably won't need the tape but continue to use it, then you can focus all your attention on relaxing rather than having to remember the instructions.

Ask someone who's voice you like the sound of to read the instructions into a tape for you, then you will always have that person rather than yourself instructing you.

When you read the instructions into the tape imagine you are doing the exercise and try to time your instructions to match its slow pace. You might also try putting some relaxing music on in the background while you are recording.

At the start of the exercise sit down in a comfortable chair with your back straight and your feet flat on the floor. Place your hands in a relaxed pose in your lap.

- Take a deep inward breath through your nose, filling your lungs and drawing the breath right down to your diaphragm.
- Breathe out, feeling your body relax as the breath flows from your mouth.
- Take another deep inward breath, filling your lungs and drawing the breath right down to your diaphragm.
- Breathe out, feeling your body relax as the breath flows from your mouth.
- Take a third deep inward breath, filling your lungs and drawing the breath right down to your diaphragm.
- Breathe out feeling your body relax as the breath flows from your mouth.

- Focus all your attention on your scalp.
- Really 'feel' your scalp and all the follicles of your hair.
- Now tense the muscles in your scalp and hold them for a slow count of seven.

- Relax the muscles in your scalp and feel the tension flow from you.

- Focus all your attention on your forehead, eyes and face.
- Really 'feel' your forehead, eyes and face.
- Now tense the muscles in your forehead, eyes and face and hold them for a slow count of seven.
- Relax the muscles in your forehead, eyes and face and feel the tension flow from you.

- Focus your attention on your shoulders and neck.
- Really 'feel' your shoulders and neck.
- Now tense all the muscles in your shoulders and neck and hold them for a slow count of seven.
- Relax the muscles in your shoulders and neck and feel the tension flow from you.

- Focus your attention on your upper chest, upper back and the tops of your arms.
- Really feel your upper chest, upper back and the tops of your arms.
- Tense all the muscles in your upper chest, upper back and the tops of your arms and hold them for a slow count of seven.
- Relax the muscles in your upper chest, upper back and the tops of your arms and feel the tension flow from you.

- Focus your attention on your forearms and hands.
- Really 'feel' your forearms and hands.
- Now tense all the muscles in your forearms and hands and hold them for a slow count of seven.
- Relax the muscles in your forearms and hands and feel the tension flow from you.

- Focus your attention on your abdomen.
- Really 'feel' your abdomen.
- Now tense all the muscles in your abdomen and hold them for a slow count of seven.
- Relax the muscles in your abdomen and feel the tension flow from you.

- Focus your attention on your lower back where it is in contact with the chair.
- Really 'feel' your lower back.
- Now tense all the muscles in your lower back and hold them for a slow count of seven.
- Relax the muscles in your lower back and feel the tension flow from you.

- Focus your attention on your pelvic area and your thighs where they are in contact with the chair.
- Really 'feel' your pelvic area and your thighs.
- Now tense all the muscles in your pelvic area and your thighs and hold them for a slow count of seven.
- Relax the muscles in your pelvic area and thighs and feel the tension flow from you.

- Focus your attention on your knees and calves.
- Really 'feel' your knees and calves.
- Now tense all the muscles in your knees and calves and hold them for a slow count of seven.
- Relax the muscles in your knees and calves and feel the tension flow from you.

- Focus your attention on your ankles, feet and toes.
- Really 'feel' your ankles, feet and toes.
- Now tense all the muscles in your ankles, feet and toes and hold them for a slow count of seven.
- Relax the muscles in your ankles, feet and toes and feel the tension flow from you.

Now sit and enjoy the feeling of peace and try to visualise a favourite place, somewhere that you like and that makes you feel relaxed and at ease. Walk along a deserted beach or stroll along a mountain path in your mind. Take a few minutes there and refresh yourself.

Now open your eyes.

Finding the opportunity to relax is important and, if we pay attention to our own energy cycle, our body will tell us when is a good time to do it. During the day there are times when we feel very sharp and alert, when we're in a Beta state and there are others when we are slower, more relaxed and moving into an Alpha state. We need to make the most of these slower Alpha times.

You may be aware of the 90-minute sleep cycle when brainwaves change from Delta (deep sleep) to the higher frequencies of Theta where active dreaming takes place and we enter REM (rapid eye movement) sleep. More recent research has identified that this 90-minute cycle also occurs when we are awake.

This 90-minute waking cycle is called the 'ultradian rest response' and is evidenced by loss of concentration, a sudden tiredness and our thinking becoming unclear. These symptoms appear to occur at approximately the same 1.5 hour frequency as when we are asleep.

You can test this hypothesis yourself very easily by identifying and taking a note of those times in the day when the symptoms appear. Maybe you suddenly feel fatigued or, after working productively for a while, you lose concentration. Perhaps you get up from your desk and go and talk to someone or fix yourself a coffee. Sometimes you just find that you have not heard the last few things people have been saying. You'll probably find that they occur at approximately 90-minute intervals.

Whether or not you accept the 'ultradian rest response' theory, we all know there are times during the day that we move into a low period, whatever we call it, when the symptoms we mentioned above appear. This is our body and mind telling us to take a break and is a natural opportunity and the perfect time to incubate our ideas. We don't mean that every 90 minutes you should stop what you are doing and think about ideas you've generated. What we *do* mean is that when one of these low moments occurs, and it is appropriate to do so, you should take a short break and rather than making yourself a coffee or going for a wander around the office, sit down and relax for five minutes. Let yourself focus on unwinding and enjoy what your body wants to be doing – nothing!

When we take this kind of opportunity to relax we increase the chances of our unconscious mind making unusual connections and therefore, as often occurs within a short time of waking, we get a new idea or an interesting variation of an existing one.

When we're using the Uccello™ Process we must make time to slow our minds down, to experience a Theta state and so make the most effective use of our unconscious. There are many ways of doing this, some of which we have noted here. The key is not to ignore this important step and simply jump straight from 'Experimenting with your thinking' to Combining ideas and information' because if we do, we deny ourselves the incredible power of our unconscious which, when we dip into it, often provides interesting and very surprising results.

'New Ideas Emerge' is Step 5 in the Uccello™ Process and at this point you should gather any new ideas in relation to your purpose which you've generated so far. In Step 6 you will combine these with other ideas and information to create unique perspectives.

6
Combine to Create Unique Perspectives

Step 6 of the Uccello™ Process

If you have been working through the book you will, by now, have made a decision about what it is that you want to create and maybe you're looking forward to producing those novel and exciting ideas that, when applied, will give you that new product, process or system. Well you won't be disappointed. If you've followed the instructions so far, you'll have collected a lot of information and perhaps challenged one or two of your mindsets and preconceptions. You'll have used some interesting and fun techniques to experiment with your thinking and to open up some new possibilities. If you've gone on to incubate these and let your unconscious mind work on them you will probably have already produced some new and very good ideas. Now we're going to ask you to hold on a little longer so that you can add these ideas to other information and ideas you've gathered to generate many more, some of which could be genuinely unique.

Taking things that already exist and combining them in different ways and for new purposes, as we have said, is the essence of creativity. This might sound too simple but, when we're talking about anything that has been created or manufactured, as opposed to having evolved in nature, these things have come about as a result of someone taking objects or thoughts or ideas that already exist and combining them in new and unusual ways. Look around you, whether you're sitting in your lounge or your office, wherever you

The Uccello™ Process For Non-Stop Creativity

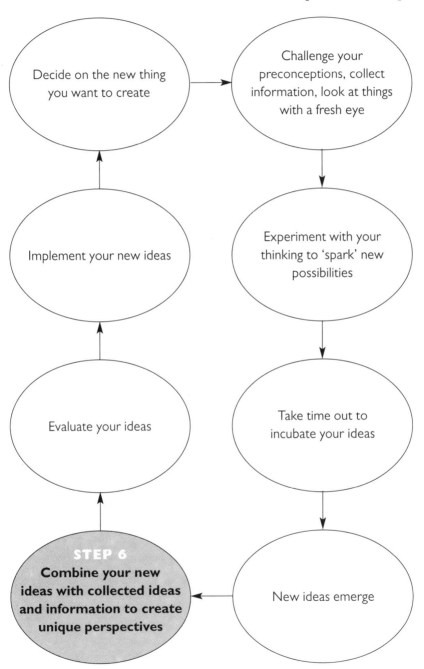

Source: Fiona McLeod and Richard Thomson, 1997.

are right now, look at all the manufactured things you can see. Can you spot the combination of elements that make them up? There is nothing manufactured that isn't a combination of existing elements, the skill is in finding the mix that will be fit for your purpose and that is genuinely new.

Because people are constantly making new discoveries in every field – science, medicine, art, technology etc. – this creates a constant and rich supply of new materials which can be used to make even more new discoveries possible. And this doesn't apply only to these areas. New things are happening and being developed every day and, in exactly the same way the inventor does, we can use any of this information to generate new combinations that produce those new products, systems, processes, whatever we want. Creativity can mean seeing things that no one else sees or seeing the same things as other people see and thinking about them differently.

We all have the capacity to be creative and, although we often don't see them as such, we make creative choices every day. When cooking, have you ever substituted one ingredient for another when you found you'd run out of the one specified in the recipe? That's a new combination and involves a creative decision. Have you ever 'cobbled together' some hardware into a kind of 'Heath Robinson contraption' to do something or to make a job easier for yourself? That's a new combination and very similar to what the inventor does.

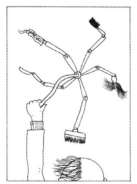

We saw in Activity 3.5 on page 42 that if we combine familiar and expected elements the result is likely to be more of the same. If we are to be really creative and inventive we must combine the unexpected and the unusual to create what is genuinely novel and different.

To be truly creative and to move away from 'more of the same' we need to stop ourselves from rushing to accept and implement our first idea. We need to be willing to put up with the uncertainty and ambiguity that not having a resolution brings. We must work at connecting things and pushing our ideas to the limit. We cannot simply accept that because we've had one good idea about how to do something we should stop there, no matter how tempting that may be.

The only means of strengthening one's intellect is to make up one's mind about nothing – to let the mind be a thoroughfare for all thought, not a select party.
                                          John Keats (poet 1795–1821)

Everyone has heard the story of Sir Isaac Newton and the apple falling on his head causing him to discover gravity. In fact, he was outside looking at the moon when he noticed an apple falling from a tree in his garden. He put these two things together, the moon and the apple falling, and it was this connection that led to his famous discovery.

How James Dyson, the inventor, came up with the idea of the cyclone vacuum cleaner is another example of putting unusual combinations together. At the time, he was actually looking for a new way to stop the air filters in his factory spray-finishing room from blocking. He heard from a friend that a nearby sawmill used a cyclone to clear the air and, when developing one for his own factory, went on to make another connection. He had found that the bags in his traditional upright vacuum cleaner at home were also constantly blocking – he connected these things (the cyclone and the vacuum) and combined the two and so the cyclone cleaner was born.

One morning, John Van Wormer a factory owner from Ohio dropped the glass milk bottle he was holding and the milk went everywhere, much to his annoyance. The incident, however, prompted him to make a connection between the newspaper he was reading and a safe container for milk. The result was the paper milk carton, an idea which he patented in 1915.

A tin pie plate from William Russell Frisbee's bakery, when put together with the imagination of flying saucer enthusiast Walter Morrison created the Frisbee.

New inventions, developments or new ways of doing things most often arise from these unusual connections, from combining one idea with other, unconnected ideas. They always come from the desire for something new, perhaps with that unscratched itch, the sand in the oyster that produces a pearl.

Imagine in the middle of the nineteenth century when all portable timepieces came in the form of pocket watches. Picture the scene – a family is gathered around the dining table and the father takes his big old pocket watch from his waistcoat pocket. Down the table his young son thinks, 'I want a watch that I can carry much easier than that'. And, as he's thinking, he notices his sister's bracelet across the table, 'That's it!' he thinks. 'All I need to do is to find a way to attach a pocket watch to a bracelet.' And so this simple combination of thoughts, this making connections, could have produced the ubiquitous wristwatch that we all wear today.

To illustrate using combining to generate ideas and to give you a picture of the process, let us recount something that happened recently. We were working with our colleagues on a project in which we were trying to find a shorthand way to describe the levels of management and leadership in organisations. Our difficulty was that we needed some kind of titles that conveyed what we meant without sounding militaristic or sexist. We also wanted to avoid any mechanistic connotations. We had thought about it and talked with each other but we hadn't quite found an appropriate answer. It wasn't our highest priority so we left it, but every now and again it came to mind and the desire to find an answer became stronger. Every so often something new would present itself as we each incubated our various ideas but, as the time drew closer when we really needed an answer, still nothing suitable had been suggested.

We got together bringing with us whatever ideas each of us had and then we had to agree what our purpose was. We knew we had to be clear exactly what we were trying to do and, after discussion, this evolved as:

We want a new way to describe the layers of management in an organisation that conveys something of the nature of the role, is easy to remember and sounds attractive.

We then noted the ideas we had already thought of, some of which included: parts of the body, the family, various versions of the captain and crew, the monarch and her court. None of these were suitable but they provided us with a very good starting point.

Hot Tip

 Use a thesaurus to generate many interesting associations before you start combining.

Using a flipchart we wrote down, under a series of headings, some of the other information we would use to start combining. Our headings were:

- This team's new ideas (in any area).
- New things that are happening in our industry.
- New things that are happening in other industries or the world at large.
- Blue sky ideas (that means whatever interests us).

We noted four or five things under each heading and then, because we wanted to start the process off with a wider range of material, we developed some associations from each. For example, one thing we noted under the heading, *New things that are happening in the world*, was: 'A cure for cancer from garden soil', which came from an item one of us had read in a newspaper some days before. We went on to make some random associations from that which included: Health – Herbal medicine – Earth mother – Medicine man – Flowers – Burial – Lawnmower.

From one of the other headings, *This team's new ideas in any area*, came 'Enhancing social capital', from which we also developed some associations that included: Village – Community – Happy workers – Productivity – Altruism – Sharing.

And we set to work . . .

In the space of ten minutes we came up with more than twenty ideas, some of which were variations on those we already had and some we hadn't thought of before. One of the ideas that was sparked off by the above combinations was to refer to the leader and the senior managers with titles that reflected their roles as members of a community who looked after the health of the organisation, a way of thinking we had previously not fully appreciated. We produced words such as 'Elder' and 'Guardian'. In a meeting later that day, we used this information to develop and push our ideas in many different directions to change the pattern of our thinking until we ultimately found something we were all happy with. As it turned out it was a further combination of the ideas we had produced.

We selected the title 'Navigator' for person at the top, because he or she is the one who sets the course and charts a safe route avoiding the metaphorical rocks, shoals and hidden dangers that might harm the organisation. The senior managers we named 'The Flight Crew' because they ensure the course is maintained and they act as a bridge between the Navigator, the crew and the passengers. These titles, while quite different from our starting point, were strongly influenced by our thoughts about safeguarding health and well-being.

Hot Tip

Supermarket shelves provide a wealth of information and ideas you can use when combining!

Combining gives us a different perspective, a new way of looking at things. Although it may seem difficult at first, with a little practice, we can become very adept. In a recent workshop, one of the participants exclaimed that we had changed the way his mind worked! We didn't – he did. In his daily life he had started collecting information from all sorts of sources he previously hadn't considered and then he put this together to generate more imaginative ideas. Serendipity, chance and our unconscious have a lot to do with it but the real work is here, in combining what we already have to create something new.

Activity 6.1 Practising combining

In Chapter 1 you combined a hat, a fish, a clock and a newspaper to make a new game. In this short activity you will use the same process to generate ideas but now we would like you to also try making associations. Use this as a warm-up exercise before you start working with the purpose you produced in Chapter 2.

Step 1
Look around you and decide on something you would like to create that could be used in the room or space you are currently in. For example: a new way to open letters, a new way to heat the room, a new way to hang pictures, a new way to store something and so on.

Step 2
Write down your purpose.

Step 3
Select any three items from the room or space around you.

Step 4
Make a series of associations from each. For example:

Pen: ink – cap – colour – fountain – draw
Shelf: book – store – tidy – reading – support and so on.

Step 5
Now combine any two or three of these to make something new. Keep focused on your purpose and try to generate ideas that will meet it. Don't worry about practicality at this stage; your aim must be to generate the largest number of ideas regardless of whether they will work. The opportunity to evaluate will come later.

Step 6
Practise putting odd and unusual things together as often as you can so as to familiarise yourself with the process and help 'loosen up' your mind.

Write the word, 'comfort' on a piece of paper and, working on your own, make as many associations as you can from it.

Ask one or two other people to do the same. Compare the results and see how many different perspectives there are.

To combine we use information from many different sources. In business, many of those who are most successful in generating ideas use a wide range of information and are constantly collecting data, news, ideas and images, all of which go into the 'melting pot' to produce new products, strategies and concepts. They don't focus on their own industry or profession but want to know what everyone is doing and what's going on in other industries, professions, countries and the world in general. The more diverse the sources the more unusual the combinations it's possible for them to make.

In Chapter 3 Activity 3.7 we asked you to collect information on ten different things that were happening in your work group or organisation, your industry or field of work, other industries and fields and the world at large. This is the start of your own information bank of data, ideas and observations that you can dip into and draw on when generating ideas. Company 'ideas banks' are a very useful, additional source of information which you can use to add to your own ideas and data.

Fast Fact *Ideas banks*

Many organisations are making use of technology to establish ideas banks, repositories where anyone in the organisation can place an idea that is then made available via Internet or intranet to everyone else in the organisation no matter where in the world they are. These ideas may be completely new, they may suggest improvements or interesting solutions to problems.

Having this rich and extensive bank of information is extremely important for the creative process. To really push the limits of our thinking and generate new and original ideas we need to use very disparate and diverse information. And, while we can make combinations in our heads, to manipulate such a large amount of data is extremely difficult. We need to write down or record information in a way that will allow us to work with it in a focused and systematic way. We might be very organised and keep a notebook especially for the purpose or we could be the kind of person who scribbles masses of notes on any surface that happens to be handy. In whatever way we store the information we need to be able to recover it easily when we want to.

When we started to develop the Uccello™ Process this is exactly the problem we faced; we needed something we could use to store information, ideas and observations that would also allow us to change and manipulate them as necessary. We designed the Uccello™ Ideas Disc for this purpose. It consists of six discs, each one larger than the next and held together at the centre so they can be rotated. Different information is written onto each disc and these can be turned to make different combinations. When we are running workshops each participant uses a Uccello™ Ideas Disc to help them generate ideas. It isn't essential that you use this particular method, what is important is that you are able to manipulate the information you've collected easily and quickly and you feel comfortable with it. You also need to think about portability. To be most effective you need to have your information bank with you all the time so that you can jot down ideas and observations whenever they occur. They may not seem particularly relevant at the time but when you look at them later it's remarkable what they can spark off and lead to.

Methods for storing information and ideas include:

- An A5 notebook to jot down ideas, information, thoughts and observations. You will also need a pen! Try using a multicoloured pen so you can make easy, visual distinctions between different pieces of information.
- 3 × 5 index cards perhaps in different colours for different kinds of information.
- Note cards – business card size is very handy for keeping in your pocket.

- A handheld cassette recorder is great for noting thoughts but retrieving them usually means you just have to write them down anyway.
- A handheld computer that you can print from. One that recognises handwritten information and transforms it into typescript is particularly useful.

Getting into the habit of noting down ideas, thoughts and observations, interesting items of information from newspapers, the media etc., is essential for anyone who is serious about generating unique ideas.

Below are some questions that we've used with our clients to help them think about the information they might use to create new and interesting combinations. Some of these you may have already answered in Chapter 3 Activity 3.7 and we've included some others that require you to think more broadly.

Activity *6.2 Collecting additional information*

 Think about how you will record and keep the information you've gathered already (notebook, index cards, etc.) then answer the following questions and write down your answers using that selected method.

- How do you spend your time differently than you did five years ago?
- How do people in society spend their time differently than they did five years ago?
- What are people spending their money on?
- What does society in this country value most?
- What is the general state of health of people in this country?
- What music is popular at the moment?
- What is the political 'complexion' of the country?
- What political changes are apparent in this country and other countries?
- What type of clothes are currently fashionable?
- What new inventions have come onto the market most recently?

- What are the most current technological, medical, scientific advances?
- What new ways of working are happening in your organisation?
- What new ways of working are happening in other organisations?
- What new ideas, concepts, innovations are occurring in industries other than your own?
- What new ideas have your team or any of your colleagues at work come up with in the last 6–12 months?
- What, currently, are the most successful types of business enterprise?
- What new products or processes have your business competitors introduced recently?
- Where in the world is the most environmental change taking place?
- What demographic changes are evident in society?
- What are the most significant changes in culture evident in society?
- What are the most significant ways in which people are changing the ways they behave?
- What is the current pattern of spending in society?

You will notice that much of the above information relates to new trends and changes, this is not a coincidence – change creates opportunity.

Once you've answered all the above questions and added these to the other information you've already collected you'll have a fairly comprehensive bank of information to work with. If you add to this daily you'll always have a rich source of current data. Also, by noting information, you will become more observant, more aware of your surroundings and will remember it more easily.

Activity *6.3 Combining in relation to your purpose*

 Having practised combining in Activity 6.1 and, having collected a large amount of information to work with, it's now time to generate ideas in connection with the purpose you wrote down in Chapter 2. Go back to it and refresh your memory. Is it still relevant? Change it if you want to but remember the guidelines for writing a purpose: it must be future oriented, it must be open enough not to limit your thinking and it must start with the words 'I want a new . . .'

Step 1
Note your purpose: what it is you want to create?

Step 2
Look at the information you have collected and select two items from it. To get started, try combining something you have come up with in Activity 6.2 under the headings '*What new ways of working are happening in your organisation?*' and '*What new clothes are currently fashionable?*'. Write these down on a sheet of paper, or, if you are using cards to record your information, simply select the cards and put them in front of you.

Step 3
Write down some associations from each, these can be single words or short phrases. Don't spend too long on associations, after all that's the easy bit!

Step 4
Look at all the words and phrases in front of you and, keeping focused on your purpose, make a note of anything they suggest to you. Work very hard at writing *all* your thoughts down. You will find yourself editing out ideas on the grounds of practicality or just because they seem plain silly, but the sillier the idea the better! Let yourself go. You will have the opportunity to properly evaluate your ideas at Step 7 in the Process.

Step 5
When you find yourself running out of ideas, select another piece of information from your 'bank' and either add it to what you have or substitute it for something you have already used. Look at the combinations it makes and note down any more ideas.

Step 6

Keep working at pushing for more and more ideas by using different combinations of two or three items of information. (We have found that to combine more than two or three takes practice so, particularly at first, keep changing the sets of information you are using.) You will get tired and may find the process difficult at first, but persevere.

Keep your list of ideas; you will use them to practise evaluating in the next chapter.

So now you've combined disparate and unusual thoughts and ideas to make something new that will, hopefully, meet your purpose. You have exercised your creativity and, having done it once, you have a method you can use again, whenever you need or want a new idea.

This then completes the creativity phase of the Uccello™ Process. You have worked through each step and we hope you have enjoyed the activities and the insights they've given you. You may be already thinking differently about what creativity is and, hopefully, your confidence in your own creative abilities has increased.

The next phase of the Uccello™ Process deals with putting your ideas into action and the first step in achieving this is to sort and evaluate your ideas.

7
Evaluate
Your Ideas

Step 7 of the Uccello™ Process

You are now at Step 7 and have reached the end of the creativity part of the Uccello™ Process. Already you've travelled a long way from that first point when you decided what you wanted your purpose to be. Now it's time to move on and test the ideas you've generated and choose the one you want to put into practice. This begins the innovation part of the process.

As we move through the Uccello™ Process, at different stages, we need to play different roles and apply different skills and ways of thinking. During the search for ideas, the role is one of creator and inventor. We need to be able to step out of our worldview, expand our mental horizons, suspend judgement and be receptive to information from a wide range of sources. We need to be flexible and tolerant of ambiguity. As we shift to making our idea a reality, however, we require a more critical focus to evaluate the creative outcomes, to develop the results and create the conditions that will allow our idea to succeed. We need to promote our idea, persuade people to share our vision and enlist their support. To succeed we have to be planners, communicators and entrepreneurs.

Step 7 of the Process is the point where we sift out and evaluate our ideas. Having worked so hard throughout the process not to evaluate, now is the point where we are actually allowed to do it! When we're generating ideas we evaluate and discard many of them, sometimes before they are even fully formulated, and we tend to express only our 'safer' thoughts. We build evaluation into the ideas generating process itself, censoring our ideas and so limiting our potential for creativity. When we are searching for ideas we have to be aware of this almost built-in reflex and actively work to prevent it kicking in. The fact that evaluation is a separate step from

The Uccello™ Process For Non-Stop Creativity

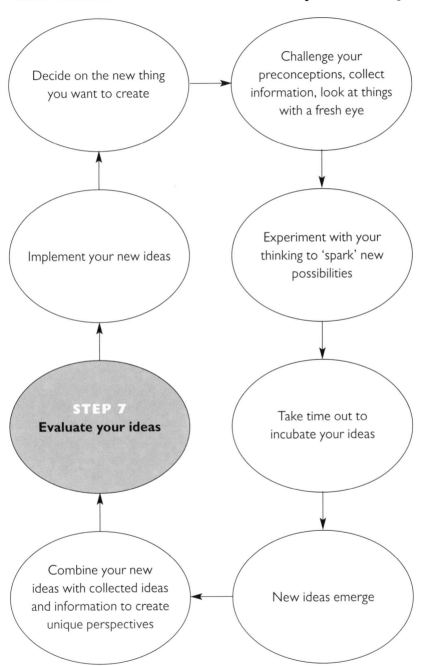

Source: Fiona McLeod and Richard Thomson, 1997.

the creative thinking part of the Process makes this easier, but we still have to work very hard to counteract it.

Now you're going to consider your ideas and choose which one you want to progress. We often find that, when people have generated a large number of creative ideas, they're not sure where to start or how to choose one they want to go with. As a result, they end up picking the easiest, the quickest, the cheapest, or the least risky to put in place. They choose the one that is safest and that they feel most comfortable with which is, in some ways, a mindset in itself. In organisations where implementation can be difficult and fear of failure is ever present, it is understandable why people make these safe choices, but we need to ask ourselves whether they are likely to be the most original or creative. The answer is usually no. Genuinely new, winning ideas usually involve a change in how people think and do things, and they are therefore likely to require time, effort, resources and perseverance if they're to be successfully implemented. So, beware of the easiest and quickest option.

Of course, we're not saying that this is always the case as an example from one of our clients in the financial services sector demonstrates. In our first workshop with them one of the groups were looking for, 'A new way to increase levels of pensions business' and they came up with an idea in relation to pensions renewals that could be implemented very quickly and easily. It was introduced immediately and is still in operation, generating substantial increased business for the company.

People often suggest 'gut feeling' or 'intuition' as a way of choosing an idea. 'Knowing without knowing how you know' as it has been called, is a way of making decisions that has not been given the same attention or credibility as analysis and rational planning. We are taught to value logical, sequential and analytical thinking above that of intuition and nowhere is this more evident than in business. However, things are changing. Intuition is beginning to be seen as important and more people are actively working to understand it and to develop their ability to think intuitively. Many famous business people readily admit to making decisions on 'gut feeling' and share their experiences of successful decisions they've made on this basis. In the decision-making process both of these have their place and many decisions benefit from using both modes at different times. Our first reaction, our 'gut feeling', can provide a good starting point which we can then go on to try and verify objectively. It's worth remembering that our next task will be to gain the agreement and support of others. Convincing them on the strength of 'gut feeling' alone is likely to prove difficult.

So what kind of things should you look for when evaluating your ideas? On what criteria should you judge them? When dealing with business or work creativity the key word is value. If you're going to introduce something successfully, either within an organisation or into the marketplace, it's not enough to have a novel idea, it has to have value to the customer or in some way help the organisation to achieve its objectives. If you can't convince people that your idea is useful and practical as well as novel then the chances are it will remain on the drawing board and never see the light of day. Creativity and innovation in a business context is the quest for the new and the *valuable*. New ideas must have direct relevance and applicability and must be customer and market led. Only then will they stand a chance of becoming innovations that deliver the added value or the competitive edge that you're looking for.

When considering and evaluating your ideas, therefore, it is essential to look at its value to people in the organisation (if you are part of one) and outside in the wider marketplace. It is also important to remember that, at the various stages of the implementation process, your idea is going to be evaluated by different people with different criteria and agendas. So, for instance, if you are part of an organisation, you might need to get the go ahead from finance, marketing and human resources all of whom will have different criteria for their evaluation. If you are going into business, your first port of call, even before your bank manager, could be your life partner, who will need to be convinced of the merits and benefits of the venture before they'll give you their support. It's essential, therefore, that when you are evaluating your ideas you take these different viewpoints into account.

There are a number of methods of evaluating ideas including decision trees, cost/benefit analysis and simply weighing up the pros and cons. We've chosen a decision grid and have customised it

My ideas	Is it likely to achieve my purpose? Max score 10	Is it new to me, my team, my organisation, the marketplace? Max score 8	How much will it contribute to achieving corporate goals? Max score 9	How much will it add value for the customer? Max score 9	What will it cost to implement? (low cost = high score) Max score 6	Do I like it? Max score 10	What is the level of risk? (low risk = high score) Max score 6	Total
1								
2								
3								
4								
5								

Figure 7.1   The decision grid

specifically for evaluating creative ideas. We selected this tool because it's very simple and flexible to use and can be adapted very effectively to creativity and innovation.

By scoring the decision grid you can compare your new ideas against one another using a set of criteria we have selected and weighted according to what we think is important when evaluating *creative* ideas. When you have completed the grid, each idea will have a total score that can act as a guide to help you make your decision. By using the grid you will be able to work through your ideas in a systematic and logical way and, because we have included a category 'Do I like it' as part of the criteria, you will also be able to bring your intuition into play and take account of your 'gut feeling'. The purpose of the grid is to help you sort out your thinking in relation to your new ideas.

Figure 7.1 illustrates the grid. We originally designed it for use in an organisational context, but at each step we make suggestions for how it can be adapted if you are a solo operator.

The decision grid

Before you move on to Activity 7.1, where you start to evaluate your ideas, we will explain each of the categories and weightings.

Is it likely to achieve my purpose?   We have included this category because clearly, if your idea fails in this first, most basic of tests there is little point in going any further. In view of its import- ance we've given it a maximum weighting of 10. As people work through the ideas generating part of the Uccello™ Process the only restriction that we constantly remind them of is: Will it meet your purpose? This is the touchstone to which you must constantly return.

Is it new to me, my team, my organisation, the marketplace? This is about assessing the novelty of the idea in the context in which you work. So, if you are trying to introduce a new system or way of working in your department, the first three, new to you, your team and your organisation will apply. If you are about to launch a product or go into business for the first time, new to you and to the marketplace are the ones to consider. We've given this category a weighting of 8 because although novelty is a key consideration when evaluating your ideas, we believe it's less important than those categories relating to value.

How much will it contribute to achieving corporate goals? The focus here is organisational and is about assessing to what extent your idea is aligned with and will help achieve the organisation's objectives. It's about measuring how valuable the idea will be to the organisation. To reflect its importance we have given it a maximum possible score of 9 because there's no point in expending time, energy and resources if your idea isn't going to take you and your organisation closer to where you want to be. (If you are an individual working on your own you could substitute: 'How much will it contribute to my achieving my overall personal and professional vision?'.)

How much will it add value for the customer?   When we refer to the customer here we mean both external customers and, if you are in an organisation, internal customers. Clearly, in the case of introducing a new product or service into the marketplace, if it isn't of use to customers or doesn't provide a better service it's not a winning idea. Similarly, if you are introducing a new system or a new way of working within your organisation and it isn't going to benefit those using it, then its value is doubtful. This category is all about value so we have given it a high weighting of 9.

What will it cost to implement?   We use the term 'cost' not only to include financial cost but also other considerations such as time to implement, relationship costs, credibility costs and anything else that might be regarded as a negative and is not taken into account in your other scoring. So, for instance, within an organisation, introducing your new idea will inevitably involve a degree of change. Some may not welcome this and so the relationship costs could be high. As we will see in Chapter 8 you can work to minimise this, but it is unlikely that you are going to eliminate it completely. Similarly, if you're considering going into business, as well as looking at the financial implications, it's important to consider the 'cost' to your family and personal relationships. Financial cost is clearly something that you have to think about carefully in any new venture, but we believe that, by their very nature, creativity and innovation inevitably involve a degree of cost that you can work to minimise but ultimately you have to accept. In view of this we have allocated it a lower score in relation to the other categories giving it a maximum potential score of 6.

Do I like it?   This is where 'gut feeling' about our ideas comes into play. Having weighed up all the pros and cons of an idea, having assessed how new it is and to what extent it creates value, if ultimately we don't like it then there is no point in choosing it and trying to implement it. To implement an idea takes energy, enthusiasm, determination and courage. It takes time and effort over what could be months, maybe years, depending on the scale of the project. If you don't like it, if you don't feel passionate about it you won't have the drive necessary to make it happen. To reflect how crucial we think this category is we have given it a maximum score of 10.

What is the level of risk?   This is about assessing the degree of risk that progressing the idea would expose you and your organisation to. There are many forms of risk: financial risk, risk to reputation, risk to status. In organisations, fear of mistakes and failure can prevent risk taking and so limit creativity and innovation. Undoubtedly, given the potential impact that mistakes can have, it is essential that you calculate risk and adjust your exposure according to your resources. But, in the pursuit of ideas, it's impossible to eliminate risk completely. In creativity and innovation a degree of calculated risk is inevitable, so we see it as less important than the other criteria. As with cost, it is essential to minimise the risk but as it is inherent in the very process itself, we have given it a weighting of 6.

It is important to stress that these categories and the weightings in particular are only intended as a guide. When you're using the grid you might want to change the categories or alter the weightings. For instance, it may be important for you to see a result in the short term, so you may want to add a category dealing with time scale. You might include, for example, 'Can it be implemented quickly?'. Also, there might be occasions when you want to consider ease of implementation so you could add 'Is it easy to implement?'. As you move through the implementation process the importance of certain categories may change at different times and you many want to adjust the cost and risk weightings according to your circumstances. Although you can change the headings and weightings, we would recommend that you use the grid in the form we present here for a while at least until you become familiar with it and feel comfortable with the evaluation process.

Activity 7.1 *Evaluating your ideas*

Step 1
From the ideas that you generated in Chapter 6 in relation to your chosen purpose, select your top five. These should be the ones that you feel are most likely to achieve your purpose, but they should also include at least one which you consider to be more radical than the others. If you are working in an organisation the ideas that you choose should be within your sphere of responsibility. They need to be things that you and perhaps your team can implement or you are unlikely to be able to make them happen.

Step 2
Fill in the left-hand column of the decision grid with your selected ideas.

Step 3
Score each individual idea under each heading. Score high for a positive response, low for a negative. For example, if you think your idea is completely original, score 8; if you think your idea could be implemented at a low cost, score 6; if the risk involved in implementing is high, score 1; etc.

Step 4
Now total the score for each idea across the columns and fill in the total score in the box on the right-hand side of the grid.

Step 5
Identify the one with the highest score and consider whether or not this really is your top idea. If you are convinced that it's the one most likely to achieve your

purpose and, most importantly, you really do like it, you can now go on and plan for its implementation.

If you are still uncertain, consider those ideas whose scores are closest to it. Is there one that rates highly and that you really want to try to implement? If so, choose it. Remember the purpose of this process is only to sort out and guide your thinking. The ultimate decision comes down to how you feel about the idea.

If, having done this you are still unsure, make a second grid, this time deleting the lowest scoring ideas and including at least one new one.

Continue this process until you have an idea that you think will meet your purpose.

Step 6
Take a few minutes to reflect on using the decision grid.

- To what extent did using the grid help you sort out your thinking?
- Was the idea with the highest score the one that you have chosen to progress? If not, why not?
- Did you end up choosing the one you liked best?
- Are you surprised by your choice? If so, why?
- To what extent did you tend to choose 'safe' ideas?
- How did the radical idea score?

Hot Tip

The purpose of including a more radical idea is to make sure that we don't immediately close down our thinking and only work with the safest ideas. Including it gives us a spectrum to work with and this helps us to position the ideas somewhere between conventional and highly unconventional. You never know it might end up being your chosen idea.

Well done! You now have an idea that you want to implement and in Chapter 8 we will take you, step by step, through how to do that.

Before moving on, however, we are going to look briefly at what to do with the remaining ideas, the ones you've not selected. Given the enormous amount of time and effort that you've just put in, it makes sense to keep them and see if they can be of use in the future or developed further.

Here are some possibilities that you might consider:

Implement more than one idea

There's no reason why you should only choose one idea. There may be several which you would like to try to implement and if there are, prioritise them and work out an action plan for each. During a recent workshop, at the evaluation stage, instead of working with five ideas, the group chose to work with ten using two decision grids. They came up with two lists, one containing ideas to be implemented immediately, i.e. in the next twelve months, the other was longer term, i.e. one to three years. Within a year they had implemented all the ideas on the short-term list and had begun working on the second, longer term one.

Build on your ideas

Bright lights file   One way you can build on your ideas is by working on them to add value and strengthen them where necessary.

Begin by working through all the ideas that you've generated and pick out those you think have potential. Make a list of these and, if you have time, use the decision grid to score them and put them into a 'Bright lights' file for the future.

Whenever you have a spare moment, select one idea and try to develop it further. What you are trying to do is to identify the weaknesses of the idea as it exists and to strengthen it. If you've already scored the idea on the decision grid then, using those scores, identify its weaknesses, i.e. where it scored badly. For instance, if the idea had a low score for 'Is it new to you, your team, your organisation, the marketplace?', then you might go back to Chapter 6 and, using the idea, work through the combining activity again. This will help you push the idea further and so increase its novelty.

If, on the other hand, you think an idea is very new but doesn't have sufficient value for the customer, try to develop it to make it more valuable. Maybe you could make it more practical and easy to use or you could reduce its cost. Also check its relevance. It might be new and practical but is it what the customer wants or needs now or in the near future? If the answer is no, then either try to make it more relevant, or, if you think that it will be more relevant longer term, keep it as a project to be tackled later.

If the idea you want to work with hasn't already been scored, then using the decision grid, score it and work through the categories adding value and developing the idea where necessary. In this way it is possible to work through all the remaining ideas.

Seed file   Another way of building on ideas is to incorporate feedback and input from other people. This is a valuable way of developing your ideas and one which you can do easily either in an organisation or as a solo operator.

Work through the ideas that you didn't select, identifying any that you think have potential and make a list of them. This will become the basis of your 'Seed file' for the future. By talking to and involving other people you can feed and grow these ideas and bring them to fruition.

Now taking a separate page for each idea, write your purpose statement at the top and your idea underneath it.

Having done that, split the page in two horizontally and head one section: 'What I like about the idea' and the other 'How can it be added to?'.

Now circulate your file among your friends and trusted colleagues and see what comes back. Someone may have been thinking along similar lines and have an idea of their own, in which case you could try combining the two ideas to see if you can increase their originality and quality. You may want to do this separately or meet face to face and work together to build on it.

How often have you had an idea and rushed excitedly to tell someone, only to be met with: 'We tried that years ago', 'It'll never work' or 'Yes, but'? New ideas are, by their nature, fragile and need to be protected and nourished, so think carefully before you share them with someone else.

Find a champion

When you're assessing the remaining ideas, if you identify one that you think is good, but is outside of your sphere of responsibility and you personally can't implement it, don't discard it. If you're working in an organisation, think about who else might be interested in it or who would be in a position to make it happen and talk to them about it. (For more about Ideas champions see Chapter 8.) Again be careful who you talk to. Organisations are full of 'idea killers'. These people are capable, not only of instantly killing your idea stone dead, but also of discouraging you from coming up with new ideas in the future.

If you are working on your own see if the idea can be simplified, adapted or altered to bring it within your sphere of influence. Alternatively, bank it for the future. You never know when your circumstances may change or external conditions might make it possible. Leonardo da Vinci came up with ideas for both a helicopter and a submarine and recorded them in his notebooks. It was only the absence of the technology at the time that prevented these groundbreaking ideas becoming reality.

We've noted here some of the ways in which you can work on and build your ideas. You can use just one or use them all. If you get into the habit of keeping ideas on the backburner, it will mean that you've always got another project which could lead to that new and original idea which will keep you ahead of the game.

8
Implementing Your New Idea

Step 8 of the Uccello™ Process

In Chapter 7 we moved from creativity into innovation. Now we're going to continue the process of turning your creative idea into a practical reality.

You might be a manager with an idea that could improve the way your department or division works or an entrepreneur with a new invention or business idea for which you need funding and support. You could be an operator in a factory with an idea about how to make things function more efficiently. Whatever your role, you need other people to buy in to your idea and become involved before it is likely to be implemented. This chapter will help you to plan for how to get that buy-in and will outline the steps you need to take for successful innovation.

Unless we happen to be the all-powerful ruler of a remote fantasy kingdom, implementing our ideas needs the involvement of other people and, unfortunately, they don't always see things our way. They don't always react the way we expect them to or do the things we would like. We cannot assume it will be obvious to everyone just how brilliant our idea is and trust that they will go along with it. Bringing them on board, getting them to buy in is vital to our success and needs to be planned.

Equally, we must not fear innovation; we mustn't be afraid that our idea will be rejected and so try to implement it quietly hoping that no one will notice. Nor should we shy away from turning our ideas into reality just because it seems like hard work. Generating creative ideas is fun, it's energising, it's motivating but when it comes to, 'how do we make it happen?' we often tend to back off. On the other hand, if we push forward and make plans that will give us the best

The Uccello™ Process For Non-Stop Creativity

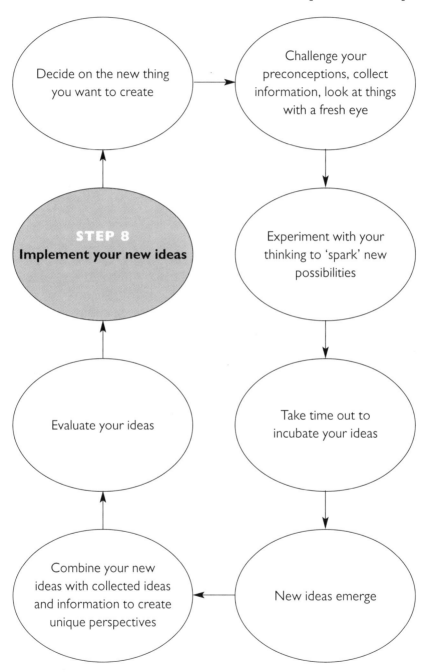

Decide on the new thing you want to create

Challenge your preconceptions, collect information, look at things with a fresh eye

STEP 8
Implement your new ideas

Experiment with your thinking to 'spark' new possibilities

Evaluate your ideas

Take time out to incubate your ideas

Combine your new ideas with collected ideas and information to create unique perspectives

New ideas emerge

Source: Fiona McLeod and Richard Thomson, 1997.

chance of success, that too is motivating and can also be a lot of fun. The real pay-off, however, is when, having thought of all the angles and executed our well-laid plans, our idea is taken on and made real. Then the feeling of achievement is extraordinary.

When we want to introduce a new idea we have to work at it. Influencing others, seeking the finance, trying out variations to make certain our idea is practical, are all part of the process. Hard work and commitment go hand in hand with innovation but perseverance can help us win through. After all:

- Thomas Edison said 'I never failed once, it just happened to be a 2000-step process'.
- Stephanie Kwolek overcame the difficulties of being a woman in a male-dominated environment to invent Kevlar.
- James Dyson spent five years developing his bagless cyclone vacuum cleaner and produced 5127 prototypes.
- Curt Herzstark continued to work on his designs despite being imprisoned in Buchenwald concentration camp and, on his release, invented the world's smallest mechanical calculator.
- Beethoven was deaf!

In organisations we've found that, once people have discovered that they can be creative and they've practised their skill, their enthusiasm and confidence are so high that they rush forward to tackle all those things that they just *know* could be done better. They get together with other like-minded people and, fired with enthusiasm, they put their new found abilities to work to produce truckloads of ideas to do things differently and to replace their least favourite systems and processes. This is great and has resulted in many, very effective ideas being implemented. Not all have been successful, however, and in almost every case, this has been due to lack of planning and a failure to get buy-in from those whose help and support were needed to turn their ideas into reality.

When we start to make plans for turning our ideas into reality we need to think about many things. Most of them are about people and how best to communicate with them and influence them. We need to appreciate people's motivation, what turns them on and what puts them off, because it's only by thinking about these things in advance that we can devise plans that will succeed. We need to think about how people deal with change. Reactions to change vary from person to person, but we can be certain that change makes the majority of people, at least initially, a little uncomfortable. Some are more receptive than others, some enjoy the element of risk taking that change brings, some are sceptical and wary to the point of almost total resistance (sometimes even before they know what the change is about). When a change involves, not just a different way of doing something, but perhaps a completely new idea altogether, then the resistance is likely to be even greater. This applies to the entrepreneur just as much as to people working in organisations. Whoever you are, whatever your situation, it isn't a question of *whether* to influence anyone but of *who* needs to be influenced and brought on board.

We need others to buy in to our idea and the benefits it will bring to them, to the organisation as a whole, to humanity or whatever is important to them. If you are an entrepreneur, the people you must influence might include:

- *Bankers and investors* who are needed to finance the development and production of an invention or new business concept.
- *Supporters* who will help put in the work during the early stages of product development.
- *Potential employees* who will need to believe they will have a future with the new operation.

If you are in an organisation you may need to influence:

- *Peers* who may have to reorganise themselves to accommodate new ways of working.
- *Employees* who will actually implement the idea and who may need to learn new skills to make it happen.
- *Managers* whose authority you need to provide resources and permission for new ways of working.
- *Financial people* who may need to amend budgets to accommodate new ways of operating.

It must be remembered that there is nothing more difficult to plan, more dangerous to manage than the creation of a new system. For the initiator has the enmity of all who would profit by the preservation of the old institution and merely lukewarm defenders in those who would gain by the new.

Nicolo Macchiavelli

If you've involved others in generating and evaluating the new idea you will have taken a major step in securing their commitment and their buy-in. They will already have some level of ownership of the idea and they are, therefore, much more likely to be interested in seeing it implemented. If, however, a new idea is yours alone you must take more people and more information into account when planning for its implementation. If those you need on board are to give their commitment to your idea you need them to understand it and the reasons behind it. They will need to know the background, why you think the change is necessary, what exactly is wrong now and how you think things will change for the better.

When people are confronted with a new system or process or a new machine or mechanism for doing an existing job, their resistance often shows itself in the form of body language. They may not actually say, 'So what?' but their closed posture and cynical expression speak volumes and are a clear sign that they'll need some convincing before they agree that what you're proposing is as wonderful as you think it is. After all, if everyone is happy enough with the way things are now, so what if you've got a new idea? Why should they change? You need to convince them that your idea is genuinely better, not just different.

The first time we introduced the Uccello™ Process to our colleagues, and even although we know each other very well and value each other's professionalism highly, we were met with the 'So What?' response – they couldn't see the benefit. Our idea was genuinely new but all we had was our own conviction that it would work and that our clients would love it. We were enthusiastic and we thought our colleagues would share that and appreciate how brilliant it was. Instead, because we didn't give them enough background and they had no experience of it, because we didn't set the scene well enough,

we were met with, 'Uh huh, but so what?!' We subsequently
brought them on board and they now share our enthusiasm. It
just took longer and was more difficult because we didn't
present our case in the best way.

To present your case in the best way you need to anticipate and take
care of the, 'So What?' response as early as possible. You can do this
by giving the audience a picture of what the future could be like for
them once the idea is in place.

In Chapter 2 when you defined your purpose we highlighted the
benefits of visualising your desired future once your idea has become
a reality. Using this vision to illustrate what life would be like for us,
for our peers, perhaps for our organisation, for whoever our idea
will affect can provide a strong counter to the 'So What?' response.
You need to communicate your vision of the future to inspire your
audience and they will be inspired if you can let them see how the
future could be better if the idea were implemented. 'Better' in this
case might be for them and their department, it might be for
society in general, it might be for financial investment, it might be
purely for the enjoyment and excitement of introducing something
new. You will get the green light if you remove the 'So what?'
response by inspiring those whose support and assistance you need.

When introducing a new idea into an organisation a 'small-win
strategy' is often best. That is, don't try to change the world in
one move or you're likely to come unstuck. You also run the risk of
alienating those you want to take with you who are unlikely to give
you a second chance if, by taking on too much, the enterprise has
become doomed to failure and with it the credibility of anyone who
gave it their support. Start small, don't try to change the world all at
once; start with your own 'back yard' or perhaps just with a corner
of it. Make small changes at first, ones that don't affect too
many people and for which you can get approval quickly and with
little effort. This way you increase your chances of success by
minimising the risk to everyone involved. Also, by introducing a
new idea for doing something that is big enough to make a difference yet small enough to get approval without too much resistance,
you can keep up the momentum people need to stay on side and

interested. When we 'win' by making our new idea a reality and those people who helped make it happen also feel what it's like to 'win', they will give us their support the next time we need to implement our next new idea and the next time and the next time . . . because winning feels good.

While a small-win strategy is often the most appropriate route for those working in organisations, for others there may only be one giant step, after all you can't leap a chasm in two jumps! Whether you go for a number of steps or one giant leap will depend on the idea and your circumstances. To succeed you must make the right choice for your own situation.

Here is a checklist of actions you may need to take. Select from the list those that are appropriate to you and your situation.

1 Picture your vision of the future and be prepared to present it to others.
2 Test out your idea with someone who is likely to understand what you are trying to do and who will challenge your thinking in a positive way.
3 Seek buy-in from those closest to you, you will need their support.
4 Identify a Champion who will help you to present your idea to important others with whom he or she has influence.
5 Identify how implementing your new idea fits with corporate strategy and will help achieve corporate goals.
6 Present your vision and seek buy-in from your work team.
7 Involve your work team in planning any presentation you may need to make in order to secure permissions, finance and other resources.
8 Make prototypes if appropriate.
9 Make a business plan for your bank and investors if appropriate.
10 Prepare a presentation that answers as many 'So what?' questions as possible.
11 Consider patenting your idea if it meets the criteria of cost effectiveness and usefulness and you have determined there is a reasonable prospect of a market for it.
12 Prepare for success!

To begin planning, the first thing you need to do is identify everyone who will be affected by your idea if it were to be implemented. This will include all those who would rather see things remain as they are as well as those who want to see things done differently. You must think about the people whose authority is needed to proceed; those people we may not necessarily want to be actively involved but whose support and approval will help assure success; those you need working alongside you throughout; and also those you need to stand back and not get involved. It's always worth considering everyone; leave no one out. Failure to take account of how someone might react to a new idea could be the one thing that limits your success in making it happen. Once you've identified these 'stakeholders' you need to think about what their reaction to the new idea will be. Will it be favourable and will they want to get involved? Do you want them involved? Will they be resistant? What in particular will they be resistant to? What can you do to minimise their resistance? The following activities will help you to answer these questions.

Activity 8.1 *Getting buy-in*

 If you've been completing the activities throughout this book you will by now have at least one idea that you want to take forward.

Step 1
Make a list below of everyone who could have an impact on whether your idea is implemented. Start with those immediately around you and work out in ever increasing circles.

Name	Action (A, B, or C)
1.	
2.	
3.	
4.	
5.	
6.	
7.	
8.	
9.	
10.	

Step 2

Under 'Action' note next to each person, whether you need him or her to:

A – Work with you directly to make your idea happen.
B – Give support for your idea but take no direct action.
C – Stand back and allow yourself and others to implement your idea unhindered.

Step 3

Think about your purpose and your vision and prepare a short introduction to illustrate to each of those named above any benefits of implementing your idea that you believe will appeal to them. Once you've completed your opening statement check it to see if it answers the 'So what?' question.

Step 4

For each person named above you have now identified the role you want them to play (involved directly, support only, not involved). Write out exactly what you would say to each in order to convince them to accept their role, think about each person's motivation and how they are likely to respond. Put this statement together with the introduction for each which you prepared at Step 3 above and you have the opening for your presentation.

If we're going to persuade people to adopt our idea we need to help them move out of their comfort zone. After all, doing things differently can be uncomfortable even when we know it's good for us and it's the right thing to do. If we've spent years doing something in a particular way we will always slip back into that comfort zone until the new way is learned and it becomes second nature. If you have ever had a lesson from a tennis or a golf coach and they advised a change in the way you stand or hold the racket, then you'll know what we're talking about. It feels all wrong and, even when you see the ball going farther and straighter, it is only too easy to go back to what feels familiar. To reduce resistance and minimise the chances of people slipping back you need to work even harder to get buy-in.

Activity 8.2 *Managing resistance*

 This exercise is a useful way to identify where someone's resistance might lie. For people to commit themselves to our new ideas, these four factors need to be present:

(a) They need to be dissatisfied with how things are now.

(b) They must like the sound of how things would be if our idea were to be implemented.

(c) They must be able to see a straightforward first step that they could take to make it happen.

(d) They need to be convinced that doing things differently will not cost them more than they are willing to pay (this could be financial, comfort, status, etc.).

For those who like numbers try the following:

Allocate either a 1 or a 0 to each of the four factors above for each person whose buy-in you seek, i.e. if you estimate that the person is definitely not happy with the way things are now – score 1, if they are happy – score 0. If you think they are likely to be inspired by how things would be if your idea were acted on – score 1, if not – score 0. If you believe you can help them to see a practical first step to make it happen – score 1, if not – score 0. If you can make it clear that the 'cost' to them is negligible – score 1 or if the cost could be high – score 0. Once you've allocated your scores multiply them (a) × (b) × (c) × (d). The answer you are looking for is 1, which you can only get if you score 1 for all four factors. If you score 0 for any, the answer will come out at 0 which indicates that you will meet resistance until you do something to change the other person's perception. You will need to work on the area or areas that scored 0 so you can remove the resistance in order to progress.

Whether we're presenting our idea to one person or to many and no matter if it's our life partner, business partner, the board of directors, the bank manager or work colleagues, there are a number of things we need to be clear about if our presentation is to be successful: the objectives, the audience, the material and the preparation.

Be clear about your objectives   That is, what you want the presentation to do. While it would be wonderful if, simply by presenting our ideas to people, they rushed immediately to give their approval and signed up there and then. In the real world, however, we have to be prepared for that not to happen. If you set your sights too high in an initial presentation you will probably talk too much and push it too far. You need to be realistic about what you can reasonably expect from the meeting. If you are clear about your objectives and set them at an achievable level you will be much more likely to pitch your presentation just right.

Many people like to think things over before they are willing or able to discuss them in detail, let alone give approval. It's worth thinking about whether the person or people to whom you are presenting might appreciate it if you were to give them some information before the meeting, setting out the key points you want to discuss with them. (Whether this information is in writing will be dictated by who you are presenting to.)

Hot Tip

 Before you go into your meeting visualise yourself getting the result you want – 'see' an enthusiastic and approving audience.

Know your audience   Completing Activity 8.2 above will give you valuable insights and will help you to adjust the presentation to provide whatever emphasis each person needs to remove his or her resistance. You need to think about your audience's priorities and preferences. What are their 'hot buttons'? What's going to make them sit up and take notice? How do they like to receive information?

Different people like information presented to them in different ways. They are broadly split into two types, those who like the 'big picture' and those who are attracted by the details. That is, some people like to know the detail before you tell them your conclusions and others want to know the conclusions first so that, when you tell them the details, they can put them in context. If you present a lot of background and detail to someone who wants the 'big picture' first, they will most likely get bored and turn off before you get the chance to tell them how great your idea is and how it will benefit them. Likewise, if you start the presentation by explaining the benefits of changing something and you are talking to someone who wants to understand the details first, you run the risk of losing them too. So think about it, does the person want you to 'cut to the chase' and give them a big picture overview (followed by the details if they are interested)? Or, does he want to build his understanding bit by bit, starting at the beginning and building up to the outcomes, conclusions and benefits? Understanding the thinking styles of your audience will help you communicate more effectively with each person. You'll get some clues about people's thinking styles by how they present information to you and others. When they are telling you something do they tend to start at the beginning with some background then, sequentially, build up the story bit by bit until they reach the conclusion? If so, then that's how you should present to them. Or, do they start with the conclusion and then explain, broadly, how they reached it? Regardless of your own preferred style, try to present according to your audience's preferences; clearly, if it's a large and mixed audience you need to vary your styles of delivery.

Know your material   Your idea is your baby and you know it well. Unfortunately, that doesn't mean you will communicate it well to other people. It's important to prepare the presentation taking account of what other people want and need to know and also how they want to hear it. Because you know the material so well there might be a tendency to say too much. You may give too much detail or perhaps not enough because you make assumptions. Structure the presentation with a clear beginning, middle and end and time it to ensure that you can say what you need to say strongly and positively in the time available. Whether the audience is one person or a hundred, their attention span will be about the same, peaking after 10 minutes and reducing over the next 30 minutes or so. If you want to keep your audience on side and attentive, involve them by asking them questions, creating as much of a dialogue as possible.

Decide the best way to showcase your idea to ensure it's listened to and the message understood. This depends as much on the audience and their needs as on the nature of the new thing you propose. If the idea lends itself to it, you might make a prototype to demonstrate it. You could, perhaps, use some form of visual aid such as data projector, overhead projector or flipchart to present information in support of your case. Depending on what the idea is, you could also have the audience do something active to allow them to experience it first hand. Thinking creatively about your presentation will enhance both it and your chances of success.

Hot Tip

Your audience will generally only remember three key points so make sure you tell them what these are right at the beginning, again in the middle and again when you close.

Prepare yourself   If you've done all that we suggest, i.e. know your objectives, your audience and your material, you've already done much to prepare yourself. However, you also need to think, not just about what you are going to say, but also how you appear to your audience. Whether or not people listen to us is affected to some extent by how we appear to them. If our appearance is off putting in any way this will limit the amount of information they will take on board. So before you rush into the boss's office full of enthusiasm about your new idea but looking like the Wreck of the Hesperus, think again. It's important to create the best impression possible and this means visually as well as with the content of any presentation. To look competent and confident you need to feel relaxed. You need to think about what to wear. Getting the balance right between dressing up like a tailor's dummy to show that you've made an effort and dressing down so you feel at ease takes a bit of practice but, if you've prepared your material thoroughly at least you'll be relaxed and you'll sound confident. To help you focus and to relax you might also try Activity 5.1 on page 69.

As well as preparing yourselves and your material, your chances of success can be increased by finding someone who will act as a Champion for your new idea. An Ideas champion is someone who understands the idea's objective, is fully committed to making it happen and has credibility and influence with whoever it is you need on your side to make it a reality. A Champion, because of his or her position or level of influence, will help you get to people who might normally be out of your reach. A Champion could be anyone – a member of the management board, someone in the work group that people look up to or perhaps a local business person. What is important is that they have influence. In the early stages of development, when you need people to listen to your idea, a Champion is invaluable. They may also be the first person to whom you tell your idea so all the rules about presentations apply. Just because you think this person is going to be receptive doesn't mean you should work less hard to communicate your idea to him or her.

Creativity and innovation can present challenges to the way people think and to the status quo. It is not unusual, therefore, that when people are presented with new ideas that are different and unfamiliar they may react strongly. If you're well prepared and have made a thorough plan to present your idea, your chances of success are increased. But remember, there are plenty of sacred cows out there that people want to protect and, though you might not know it, implementing your idea could be the very thing that would consign one of them to sacred cow heaven. It's useful, therefore, in meetings where you're discussing your idea with stakeholders to have a Champion or some other suitable person act as facilitator. They will be able to recognise this potential difficulty, manage any disagreement and so minimise conflict. It is also good practice before the session starts (depending of course on who the meeting is with) to agree some ground rules for how it should be conducted. One ground rule we've found invaluable is agreeing with people that they try to recognise their natural resistance to change and suspend judgement. We encourage people in meetings to be 'Yes and . . .' rather than 'Yes but . . .' people. We insist that, when they feel themselves about to say something that blocks thinking rather than builds on it, they make a conscious effort not to simply disagree, but to try to develop the idea further.

In this chapter we've looked at the practicalities of implementing ideas, and whether you are an inventor, a manager, a craftsperson, a business leader or simply someone who wants to generate creative ideas and see them implemented, if you follow our guidance your new idea has an excellent chance of becoming a reality.

You've now completed your journey. We hope that what you've read, learned and experienced on the way has inspired you and given you insights into the creative and innovative process. Keep practising, success awaits you.

9
Using the Uccello™ Process in Your Personal Life

So far we've been focusing on how you can develop your creative thinking and innovative skills and how these can be applied in a work or business context. Now we're going to look at using them to achieve the results you want in your personal life. Whatever you want new ideas for, you can apply the Uccello™ Process. It can be used for those big, life-changing projects as well as in all sorts of little ways to change and improve whatever you do. If you're planning what to do on vacation, if you want to find a new job, if you're working out how to get more money or simply how to create more time in your life, using the Process will help you get there.

The key is to start where you feel comfortable. Remember the small-win strategy in Chapter 8. Start with something small that you can be fairly sure of achieving and build up to bigger projects. Whether it's large or small scale, the process is the same. Beginning this way will also help build your confidence. With each small success, the more confident you'll become and the more ready and equipped you'll feel to take on those major projects. What's important is making a start, following it through and then enjoying the sense of achievement this brings.

We hope that the insights and suggestions we offer in this chapter will open up new possibilities and opportunities for you and help make creativity 'just something you do', a regular part of your life. We will also be giving you some *True stories* of the Process in action to show you how other people have used it to change aspects of their lives. We hope that these will guide, encourage and inspire you.

Start by spending a moment thinking about what creativity means for you in your personal life. Do you think of it as something only other people do? Throughout the book we've emphasised that creativity isn't just about being a musician, an artist or a writer. We all have the ability to be creative and we regularly make creative choices and decisions. We decorate, we garden, we cook, we play sport and we have hobbies. Whether or not we consider them as creative is, however, another matter. These things all involve a level of creative decision making. Take sport as an example. If you watch someone playing football, you will see that they have a skill, a proficiency that allows them to strike the ball, control and place it. But they also think creatively about what they do. What makes a good player is being able to spot opportunities and, from the huge repertoire of moves possible, they instinctively put together, in their head, a winning combination that they then execute and use to beat their opponents.

Creativity is about re-arranging and combining existing things to form something new and the challenge is to make these combinations as imaginative as possible. Take clothes, for example. Fashion has always been used as a way of expressing our individuality and it is the choices that people make, the imaginative things they put together that demonstrates their creativity. Having the confidence to try things out, experiment and make the decision about what works is the creative process in action.

If you want be more creative in your day-to-day activities, using the Uccello™ Process can help you. This applies to anyone, whoever you are and however you spend your time. By developing your creative and innovative skills you can become better at whatever it is you want to do and the quality of your life will be enriched.

In our experience, people often think they have no time or opportunity for creativity. For those in employment, time spent not working is usually filled with domestic chores or family commitments. For many, the stresses of the job are so great that time not at work is thought of as simply relaxation time, so they do as little as possible. In these circumstances people see themselves as having little or no opportunity for 'self' and self-development.

For other people, the restrictions they put in place can take different forms. They could think that they are not sufficiently educated to be creative, that they don't have access to the necessary resources or it might be that they don't believe that creativity is something that 'ordinary' people do. But it doesn't matter what the circumstances, whether you're unemployed, a single parent, retired, a prime carer or an executive, the opportunity is there to develop your creativity and use it to open up possibilities and improve the quality of your life.

We are now going to take you briefly through the Uccello™ Process looking at how, in your personal life, applying each step can enhance your creative and innovative skills. We've found that using the Uccello™ Process provides people with structure and discipline for the way in which they approach coming up with new ideas. It helps them push their thinking further and apply themselves seriously to achieving what they want. It enables them to generate ideas that are truly theirs and make these a reality.

True stories 1

A retired man in his mid-sixties, after an initial period of enjoying not having to go to work, began to get restless, missing the challenge, the sense of achievement and the social inter-action that being at work had given him.

The purpose statement he came up with was:

I want a new way to spend my time that is enjoyable and fulfilling.

He used the 'Re-defining' technique to experiment with his thinking and went on to re-define his purpose as:

I want a new way to feel good about myself.
I want a new way to live life to the full.
I want a new way not to be retired.
I want a new and satisfying way to be active.

The last two definitions in particular sparked off a whole range of ideas including: do community work, take a course, find a part-time job.

Having done that, he took the information he'd already gathered at Step 2 of the Process and began combining. From the category, 'What new things are my friends and family involved in?' (see page 129), he took: Forestry (his son had recently begun a job with the Forestry Commission); University (his grand-daughter had just begun a degree); Hip replacement (his friend had just had a hip replacement).

From 'Blue sky ideas' he took: Music – Sport – Gardening – D.I.Y.

He chose to work with two of these: forestry and sport and began by making associations. From Forestry came: Growing – Nature – Environment – Wood.

And from Sport came: Football – Supporters club – Stadium.

He went on to generate a whole series of ideas from these associations.

When he was combining the words Wood and Stadium, one of the ideas he came up with was 'build a stadium'. Now it so happened that the local youth football team desperately needed new facilities for the players but did not have sufficient funds to build them. He decided that he would raise money to help them. At a later date, he used the Process again to generate creative fundraising ideas and came up with a range of ideas including 'sponsor a brick' and a 'sponsored turf walk'.

At the time of writing this the club, with his help, are well on the way to reaching their target to build the new facilities.

Using the Uccello™ Process in Your Personal Life

Step 1: Decide what you want

As we saw in Chapter 2, Step 1 is all about deciding what it is you want and it's just as important to do this when you're working with the Uccello™ Process in your personal life as it is in a work context.

Working through the activities in Chapter 2 will help you to focus on, think about and decide what it is you want to do. Whatever your venture is, whether it's a small task or a major project, it's important to know where you want to go, what your desired destination is. You have to commit yourself to the task and set up that creative tension within yourself, otherwise your desire to do something will remain just that, an unfulfilled dream.

You need your purpose to give form to what you want to do, but not to be too restrictive; don't put too many limitations on it. For instance, if you were to write down your purpose and it had to do with a new idea for a vacation you might say: 'I want to find a new way to spend my vacation that is relaxing, stimulating and exposes me to new experiences'. Already, you can see that just by wording your purpose in this way encourages you to come up with ideas that are not about going to the same place you go to every year and, wherever you choose, it must have a range of things to do that doesn't involve only beaches and sunbathing – unless, of course, you've never done that before!

If you want to change and redecorate a room in your house you might say: 'I want a new way of creating a space in which I can relax and do the things I want to do'. Again, it gives direction, says what is important to you and gives a sense of how you want the end result to be.

Or, say you've always enjoyed visiting art galleries and decide that you want to try to create something artistic yourself. You might word your purpose as: 'I want to a new way to communicate my ideas to people in a visual form'. This doesn't say what the subject will be or the medium you are going to use. It could be about anything and take the form of a painting, a sculpture, a collage, photographs, a video, topiary or whatever. By wording your purpose in this way you have specified that, for you, it's not only about the enjoyment of doing it, but about communicating with other people as well.

By deciding on something for which you want a new idea and by working at formulating your purpose statement, the chances are that, already, you will have the kind of focus and direction that is usually only applied to coming up with work and business ideas. Also, not only will you have enlisted the help of your conscious mind, this process will also have activated your unconscious in the search for new ideas.

Step 2: The preparation stage

In Chapter 3 we saw how Step 2 in the process helps to develop the right frame of mind to be creative. When we're involved in a specific project and we're searching for a new idea for something, this step takes on an intensity that fuels the process. It's also about the way we experience the world and about developing a way of life that enhances our creativity.

In that chapter we also talked about curiosity and the need, as adults, to try to rediscover the freshness and inquisitiveness that children have. If you've ever been for a walk in the country with someone who has that openness, you'll know exactly what we mean. Watching the way they experience the natural environment is fascinating. They're observant and notice everything: the flowers, wildlife, textures, colours and smells. They constantly ask questions and try to find out as much as possible. They're completely involved in what's happening and are fully 'in the moment'. Developing this frame of mind and way of looking at the world will increase your powers of observation, your ability to be creative and your appreciation of life.

The essence of this step is about being interested and attuned to what's going on in the world. We all know or have heard of people who are aged 70 or 80 but who still have that drive and enthusiasm for life. They stay that way by constantly trying new experiences and taking on new challenges. It's about keeping your thinking fresh. If you think opera isn't for you, try it. If you think going to a museum isn't interesting, visit one. If you think computers are beyond you, go to a computer class. Go to a different place for your vacation. Take up a new hobby or interest. All these activities, as well as broadening your horizons, will take you into new situations, give you new information and bring you into contact with different types of people. If you give yourself up to it, creativity will open new doors and take you to places and destinations that you've never visited before. This is lifelong learning in its finest form!

An activity we've found works very well in helping people develop this way of life is keeping a diary. This could take the form of a written journal or a scrapbook, it could be recorded on an audio cassette player or it could be a visual record – whatever works for you. Just by having to think about and record what has happened to you during each day and what has gone on in the world around you, will make you become more aware. In our experience many people get hooked on and enjoy the process so much that they begin to use it more and more creatively. They start to express themselves more freely, incorporating their opinions and comments. Also, the way they keep their journal becomes more adventurous and more imaginative as their subject matter broadens.

Try it and see how it helps you. An excellent time to start is when you're travelling or on vacation. Not only do you have more time to do it, but you're out of your normal environment and routine, meeting different people and experiencing different ways of life and cultures.

The other part of Step 2 is collecting information and, if you want to be more creative and more individual in your personal life, then the more you observe what's going on around you, the richer the bank of information you're working with, the more likely it is that you'll be able to generate imaginative and original ideas.

Say, you want to redesign your kitchen, where could you collect information from? You could go to a shop specialising in fitted kitchens, pick up some brochures and choose one from the options available. But what if you decided you wanted something more individual, something that better reflected your personality. What else could you do? If you had endless funds you could employ an interior designer, but if you don't and you want the personal satisfaction of taking on the challenge of finding something new yourself, then collecting information will give you the building blocks you need to work with.

One place to start might be to look at kitchens from different eras, such as from the 1930s or 1950s or from different countries to see if there is anything that inspires you. You could visit catering and kitchen shops to find out what's on the market; you might go to salvage yards to look at sinks, pieces of marble and furniture that could be turned into cupboards, units, tables etc. Try to find shapes, objects or textures that you like, either manufactured or in nature – these might suggest a theme around which you could design your room. Look at the colours other people have put together; find combinations that you like. Next time you're at the supermarket or out shopping, take a look at the labels and packaging and note the colours and designs. See if there's anything that sparks off an idea for a colour combination you could use. Look at magazines and books and not just those specialising in design. Remember you can get ideas from any source and, whatever you're reading or looking at, your mind will be working and your purpose guiding you. So, when you're flicking through the newspaper or you're at work or on the subway an exciting colour combination could jump out at you. And lastly, talk to anyone whose taste in design you like; the conversation could spark off a whole range of new possibilities.

If you do these things you will have a rich bank of ideas and information that you can start to experiment with and combine in new and imaginative ways. The first time you try working this way it might feel strange, uncomfortable and perhaps a bit laborious, but the more you do it, the easier it will become and the more confident you will feel. It will begin to be 'just the way you do things'.

Obviously redesigning your kitchen is a big undertaking so you might want to go for a small-win strategy. Choose something manageable and less risky and build up from there. It's interesting that people are much more likely to be creative and take risks with their children's bedrooms than their lounge!

Step 3: Experiment with your thinking

Giving yourself time and space to play with your ideas and your thinking can suggest whole new ways of looking at your purpose. In our personal lives the chances are that the majority of our time is spent with family or friends we know well and with whom we feel comfortable. In this environment our ideas and way of thinking are likely to be reinforced rather than challenged, so it's probably more difficult to see things from radically different perspectives and viewpoints. Consciously using the techniques in Chapter 4 will help you break out of this and will suggest new ways of thinking about your purpose.

All the techniques described in Chapter 4 will work well in helping you to explore your purpose. We would suggest that you use more than one and, whenever possible, spend some time experimenting with 'Metaphor'. As a technique, 'Metaphor' is highly creative and can enable you to access images and ideas that are particularly imaginative. In our experience people find it both stimulating and liberating.

True Stories 2 shows how, using creative thinking techniques, helped one of our clients to twist and push their thinking to spark off ideas that they then took on and developed further.

True Stories 2

The client was a self-employed tradesman whose company offered a range of services including painting and decorating and joinery. Like many self-employed people he spent virtually all his time working and didn't devote as much time to thinking creatively about his own life as he did to developing his business. He was keen, therefore, to use the Uccello™ Process to give him the focus and the discipline he felt he needed to look outside his work and concentrate specifically on himself and his personal life and push his thinking in new directions. He was interested in buying a new property. He already owned an apartment, which he felt was too small and didn't provide the right physical environment to be able to do the things that he thought would help develop his creativity and make new openings for him. He decided that his purpose was: 'I want to create a new living space for myself where I can do the things I want to do'.

He then went on and wrote his diary at a point three years in the future and the results were very revealing. He wrote about being able to get away from work, about separating work and personal life and having time to do other things. This brought home to him just how different his current life style was compared with how he wanted it to be. It started him thinking more about where his living space should be (he had always assumed that it would be close to his workshops).

Then he worked with several of the techniques in Step 4 including 'Opposites'. He focused on the opposite of 'living space' and came up with: 'I want to create a new working space for the future'. So he went through how he might do that and came up with buying a commercial property, converting a warehouse etc.

He then looked for a metaphor for his purpose and came up with a piece of jazz music. The associations he explored were: it was modern and fairly minimalist; it had a basic form and structure, but there was also space for individual improvisation; the atmosphere was very mellow, very cool and so on.

Then he went on to combine the information he had gathered at Step 2 and chose two areas to work with: *My new ideas* and *Blue sky ideas*. His own ideas were: Buy the apartment next door; Buy a church; Buy a bigger apartment; Convert a warehouse (from Step 3).

His *Blue sky ideas* were: Animals – Morals – Chaos – Maths – Conscience

He selected 'Convert a warehouse' and 'Maths' from his lists and made associations from them including, from Convert a warehouse: Industrial – Utility – Functional.

From Maths: Logic – System – Grids.

He then went on to combine these and came up with numerous ideas including building a basic industrial type structure designed on a grid system. He went on and developed this further and came up with the idea of a new building using girders and clad in sheets of metal, very similar to that used in commercial properties. Thinking back to his diary he decided to buy a small piece of land on the outskirts of the city and, wanting to explore this idea further, he took another item from his *Blue sky ideas* which was 'Animals'. The associations he came up with from this were: Wild – Natural – Legs.

As a result of this he decided to put the structure on stilts and to use a lot of glass to blend in more with the environment and improve the view. He went on to produce an action plan, he successfully raised the finance, bought the piece of land, obtained planning permission and is now in the process of building it.

Step 4: Incubating your ideas

Taking time out to incubate your ideas is an essential part of the process. Divert your attention from the thing you are working on so that you can access your unconscious and allow those unusual combinations to surface. Have a shower, go for a cycle, go swimming, clean your house – anything that you can do without much thought and that will absorb you. This is about giving time and space to developing your ideas and we guarantee you'll emerge from it with at least one new one, which takes care of Step 5 in the Process, *New Ideas Emerge*.

Step 6: Combining to create unique perspectives

As we saw in Chapter 6, the process of combining your own ideas with those of other people and with information that you've gathered is what really makes a difference to the originality and creativity of your ideas. In Chapter 3 we looked at a number of different sources for those ideas and information most of which will work well with a purpose in your personal life. However, here are some suggestions for you to work with. We have altered the original headings and added a few that might prove helpful:

- My new idea relating to my purpose.
- My friends' and family's new ideas (about anything).
- What new things are my friends and family involved in?
- What new things are happening in my neighbourhood/ city/town?
- What new things are happening in the world?
- What new things are happening in business?
- Blue sky ideas.

As we've emphasised throughout this book, by using this information to make unusual combinations and connections, you will be able to produce imaginative and highly original ideas.

Step 7: Evaluating your ideas

Whether you are working on a purpose in your personal life or your professional life, evaluating ideas is equally as important but the criteria and the weightings you give them might be different. Here are some suggestions for evaluating personal life ideas which you can substitute for those on the decision grid on page 94.

- Does it meet my purpose?
- How new is it to me?
- Is it within my budget?
- Will it meet my timescale?
- What is the level of risk?
- Do I like it?
- How easy is it to do?

You might want to weight budget and level of risk higher and, depending on what you are doing, timescale could be important.

Step 8: Implement your ideas

Planning carefully how to make your idea happen will increase the likelihood of it becoming a reality. Thinking in detail about those you might have to influence; how, if you need finance, you will raise it and how you are going to enlist people's help and support can mean the difference between success and failure. Applying this approach to projects will result in more and greater successes.

True Stories 3

For a long time a woman, who worked as a clerk in a bank, had wanted to write a book. She was bringing up a young family and had limited time for herself. Since she was a teenager she had harboured a deep desire to write and had written essays at school and letters to Donnie Osmond, her teenage idol! Over the years she had several ideas but had never really applied herself to writing in any consistent way. She lacked confidence and was unsure as to whether the themes she was coming up with were of sufficient interest. When we met her, the only thing she was writing were technical reports for her job.

We worked through the process in detail with her. We started with her purpose statement. At first she said she wanted to write a book but then, when she went on to think about it, she decided that the wording should be: 'I want a new way to express myself and communicate my ideas in a way that will connect with my audience'.

She then went on to imagine her life once her purpose was achieved. Rather aptly she wrote a diary focusing on a time three years from that date and it was clear from the content and style of her writing that she did indeed have a vivid imagination.

Then she used the technique 'What's not there?' and came up with: Essays – Letters – A novel – A play.

While she was working through this, she made a very interesting association in relation to how she expressed herself: 'she' wasn't there. Although we weren't quite sure what she meant, it seemed significant, so we suggested she note it down.

When she came to combine she used some items from above: Essays – Novel – Letters.

And added these to her 'Blue sky ideas' which were: Feep fit – Cooking – Newspapers – Hollywood.

She selected Letters and Hollywood from these lists and went on to make associations from these that included friends, bills and, interestingly, 'me'. From Hollywood her associations were films, stars and comic strip. She played about with the idea of making a film about her friends, or about someone called Bill! Then she moved on and started working with the idea of a comic strip. She put this together with 'me' and came up with the idea of producing a comic strip with herself as the central character. It turned out that she had always enjoyed doodling, but had never seen it as anything more than that. When she thought about it, however, the idea of writing and drawing together really appealed to her. Now, whenever she has a moment, she works on the comic strip featuring herself, which she's planning to try to sell to a magazine or a publisher.

We hope these *True Stories* have given you some ideas for how you can use the Uccello™ Process in your personal life and that you can take something from each step and make it work for you. Fundamentally, it's about a new way of thinking, both about the world and about yourself. It's about understanding how to put new ideas together and having the confidence to do it. Feeling free enough to experiment and ask yourself 'Could I try this here?' and 'What would happen if I did?' It's about trusting in your own choices and creative decisions. So whether you're cooking a meal, choosing an outfit, designing a room or looking for an idea which will help transform your life, using the Process will help you.

10

Group and Team Creativity and Innovation

If you work alone you may think this bit of the book isn't for you but don't go just yet. Sometimes, even though we're able to produce some very good ideas on our own, working with other people can often make those ideas better and more original. Also, when it comes to putting them into practice we will, almost certainly, want to involve others. Whether it's a group of friends or your colleagues at work, this chapter will show you when working with a group is practical and how it can add value to your creativity and innovation. Our focus in this chapter is on how the Uccello™ Process can be used in groups and teams and, to help you, we've adapted many of the activities that appear in earlier chapters. These can be used if you are a solo operator carrying out the activities with one or more people or if you work in an organisation.

If you are planning to introduce your work group to the Uccello™ Process, go slowly and treat them gently. Some people are, initially, quite uncomfortable with the idea of creativity. For example, they may have preconceived notions about what creativity is, how and where it can or should be used, even whether it's the kind of thing 'professional' people should be doing! Before you try any of the activities with your colleagues read what we say in Chapter 8 about getting buy-in. Present creativity and innovation to your group in a way that engages them and answers any, 'So what?' or, 'What's in it for us?' questions they may have. Much as you might want to get straight into the challenge of generating ideas, if you go too fast and don't explain fully what you want to do and why you want to do it, the results will not be good. Give them some background and illustrate, with real examples, what they could generate ideas about. Let them see the benefits of finding new ways of working or of developing new products or processes. Tell them that you will take them through a process that they can learn to use to develop their creativity. But go slowly, take it one step at a time and cover the whole of the Uccello™ Process.

Some of the activities we include here can be run as stand-alone workshops for developing specific skills and others are best combined into a more extensive session. For a new group, unfamiliar with the creative process, you can run all the activities as a complete workshop over, say, two days. To get the best results we recommend that you use a skilled facilitator who is knowledgeable about creativity and innovation, who has credibility and is trusted by the group.

You need to think about the room in which you will run the activities. It needs to be large enough for people to move around, work at flipcharts and feel relaxed. It should also have plenty of space for putting up the many sheets of flipchart paper that will be produced when the group starts generating ideas. We find that seating people in groups of four at round tables works best and gives the facilitator the opportunity to change the membership of the groups easily as the need arises. You might also think about using background music. We use classical music (you get less requests that way) and we vary the volume and pace according to the activity. Music also shows people that this is not the same as their usual work and thinking differently is the order of the day.

Group Activity 1: An introduction to combining

This activity is an excellent warm up and shows that combining the unusual and the unexpected produces original results.

Aim of the activity
To illustrate quickly and with impact how combining is the essence of creativity and that anyone can do it.

Group size
Approximately eight participants to one facilitator. The group should be split into sub-groups of four people.

Resources
A flipchart and pad for each sub-group and one for the facilitator. Flipchart pens.

Time required
15–20 minutes.

Process

1 The facilitator tells the group that this is a 'warm up' exercise to introduce them to creativity.
2 The group is instructed to work in their sub-groups to invent a new game and are told that the only rule is, they can *only* use these four items: a *hat*, a *fish*, a *clock* and a *newspaper*.
3 The group are told that they have 10 minutes and they should record their thoughts on their flipcharts.
4 After 10 minutes the facilitator asks each sub-group for one of their ideas and continues until all or almost all the possible games have been presented.
5 The facilitator leads a discussion that draws out the following key points:

  ▪ Combining unusual and unconnected items creates interesting and potentially unique results. When we work with things that are completely unconnected we are more likely to produce original ideas rather than simply variations of what we have seen or experienced before.
  ▪ We tend to evaluate our ideas in our heads before we even say them and this leads to safe and limited thinking. We are reluctant to speak our ideas out loud until someone else says something out of the ordinary that makes it OK. Once we relax we take more risks and are more creative.
  ▪ The process of combining unusual items to make something new is fun when we relax into it.

6 The facilitator congratulates the group on their ideas. She defines creativity and innovation, highlighting the difference between them and reinforces with the group that what they have been doing is the essence of creativity.

(See Chapter 1 for more information.)

Group Activity 2: Writing a purpose statement

This activity introduces the first step in the Uccello™ Process. It can be used as a stand-alone activity or as part of a larger programme. It helps focus on what it is you want and encourages you to explore it in detail. The activity ensures that, where people have different opinions and values, they agree their purpose before going on to generate ideas. As they talk about it and share their views the purpose becomes clearer and often richer for everyone.

Aim of the activity
To practise writing a focused purpose statement and so increase the chances of producing more creative ways of successfully meeting their purpose.

Group size
Approximately eight participants to one facilitator. The group should be split into sub-groups of four people.

Resources
A flipchart and pad for each sub-group and one for the facilitator. Flipchart pens. Pen and paper for each participant.

Time required
One hour.

Process
1 The facilitator introduces the purpose as the first step and the driver for the entire Uccello™ Process. He tells the group that before they start to generate ideas they must be clear about their purpose and this activity will give them the opportunity to remove any ambiguities and differences of opinion before proceeding further.
2 The facilitator asks the group to:

■ Discuss and decide upon a common purpose for their group

and then to

■ Work alone for five minutes to write a statement that encapsulates that purpose and which starts with the words 'We want a new . . .'

3 Within their sub-group each person shares his or her statement with the other group members.

4 Each group works together for approximately 20–30 minutes to agree a form of words (starting with 'We want a new . . .') that accurately describes what it is they want.

5 Each group reads out and explains their purpose statement.

6 The facilitator leads a discussion that draws out the following key points:

  ▪ An accurately written purpose statement focuses on the future and not the past.

  ▪ It always starts with the words 'We want a new . . .' to push people into thinking about new ways of doing things and not simply variations on a theme.

7 The facilitator asks the group members how their thinking changed from the beginning of the activity to the end and to identify the benefits of going through the process of agreeing a purpose and writing it down.

8 The facilitator tells participants to keep a note of their purpose as they will use it again in subsequent activities.

(See Chapter 2 for more information. See also the 'warm up' activity on pages 19–20.)

Group Activity 3: Visualising

This can be run as a stand-alone activity or integrated with others in a larger programme. It introduces people to visualising as a technique for engaging the imagination and as an aid to achieving their purpose. It involves identifying their purpose, visualising a time in the future when it has already happened and imagining the benefits its achievement has brought. Visualising is a powerful addition to the purpose statement as a driver for the creative process.

Aim of the activity

To give the group an opportunity to use their imagination in enriching their purpose statement.

Group size
Approximately eight participants to one facilitator. The group should be split into sub-groups of four people.

Resources
Pens and paper for each participant.

Time required
30 minutes.

Process
1 The facilitator reads the aim of the activity to the participants and tells them that they are about to do some focused daydreaming.
2 The facilitator asks participants to:

- Think about their purpose (see Group Activity 2) and to imagine what life would be like for them if it were already a reality.

- Select a date in the future when their purpose is in place and imagine themselves at that future time. For example, they might think about how old they will be; if they have children, what will they be doing, and so on as a help to activate their imagination.

- Assume it has already happened and not to consider how it came about, that will come later. (Participants may have to be told to avoid getting caught up in the mechanics of how it will happen.)

- Close their eyes and imagine they are in a cinema, watching a movie of their life on their selected date in the future once their purpose has been achieved. If the group work together and they will be pursuing a common purpose, they might imagine their colleagues as characters in their movie. What are they doing? What are they saying? (Participants should be reassured that nothing will happen to them while their eyes are closed and the facilitator should not move around.) (5 minutes)

- Open their eyes and wait for a moment or two to allow them to re-orientate.

- Write down the key points that they saw in their 'movie'.
- Share their 'movie' with the others in their group.

3 The facilitator leads a discussion and draws out the following key points:

- Visualising acts as a focus and a motivator.
- The images created can be recalled at any time acting as reminders of what we want and almost pulling us towards that goal.

(See Chapter 2 for more information.)

Group Activity 4: Seeing things afresh

This activity introduces the second step in the Uccello™ Process. It can be used as a stand-alone activity or as part of a larger programme and can be done by individuals in their own homes (see page 29) or in a work setting. At home, it's a great activity to involve children in as a way of developing their ability to be observant and also to help you see things through their, more innocent, eyes. You might think about asking the group to do the activity at home and to bring the results to a subsequent session for debriefing. Alternatively, if it's practical, follow the process below.

Aim of the activity

To open up and challenge people's awareness of their surroundings and to demonstrate how much more we can see when we take the time to look.

Group size

Unlimited. Participants work individually.

Resources

List of questions (see below). Pens and paper for all participants (or portable tape recorders if possible).

Time required

30 minutes.

Process

1 The facilitator reads the aims of the activity to the group and explains that creative people tend to be very observant and have the ability to see even familiar objects with a fresh eye.

2 The facilitator asks each person to go to a part of the building they are very familiar with, for example the reception area, their office, the staff restaurant, the car park etc. and once they are there, to spend a few minutes relaxing, clearing their minds and beginning to focus on their surroundings. They are told to look very carefully at what they see there, concentrating on every detail. They should consider the following questions and record their answers.

   ▧ What does the space look like from the outside?
   ▧ What is the overall impression when you walk in?
   ▧ Looking at every surface and, without touching anything, what do you see?
   ▧ If it's a public space, what signs are there and what do they say?
   ▧ What noises can you hear?
   ▧ What does the space say about those who use it?

3 Participants are told to return in 15 minutes.

4 Once everyone has returned, the facilitator asks for examples of what each person saw: the décor, the state of repair, what they discovered about the space and what they saw that was unexpected or surprised them.

5 The facilitator leads a discussion and draws out the following key points:

   ▧ Consciously focusing on every detail of a space changes the way we perceive it.
   ▧ Being observant and looking differently at things prepares the mind for creativity by opening it up to chance encounters it might have otherwise missed.

(See Chapter 3 for more information.)

Group Activity 5: Preconceptions and mindsets

This activity focuses on Step 2 of the Uccello™ Process and is about challenging the way we get locked into ways of thinking that hinder our creativity. It can be run as a stand-alone activity or as part of a larger programme. If you are working as a solo operator and have involved some others to help you with generating ideas this is an excellent way of getting them to challenge their mindsets before you go any further.

Aim of the activity
To challenge participants' mindsets and give them the opportunity to see that all is not as it seems.

Group size
Unlimited. Participants work individually.

Resources
A picture of the Uccello Clock (see page 36). Pens and paper for participants.

Time required
10–15 minutes.

Process
1 The facilitator introduces the activity with a brief talk about mindsets and being locked into particular ways of thinking and how these affect the creative process.
2 The facilitator asks the participants to think of a mechanical clock and picture it in their minds. He then asks:
   (a) How many hands does it have?
   (b) How many numbers on the face?
   (c) In what direction do the hands travel?
   (The usual answers are 2 or 3, 12 and clockwise.)
3 The facilitator shows the participants a picture of the Uccello Clock and tells them that this clock works using a system that was popular in the middle ages which tells the time by the number of hours from sunrise to sunset. It has many hands, 24 numbers on the face and, most interestingly, the hands go backwards.

4 The facilitator leads a discussion and asks the participants to:

- Comment on the implications of mindsets, e.g. who says moving round a circle from left to right is clockwise?
- Give other examples of ways of thinking that they and others have become locked into.
- Comment on the effect of becoming locked into a particular way of thinking and how it affects people's ability to think creatively.
- Say what they think they can do to limit the extent to which they suffer from lock in.

(See Chapter 3 for more information.)

Group Activity 6: Suspending judgement

This activity develops Step 2 of the Uccello™ Process and builds on Activities 4 and 5 where we saw that the more we can open up our minds and the more observant we are, the more creative we'll become. In this activity we look at what happens when we stop ourselves jumping to quick solutions and go on to push our thinking further. It can be run as a stand-alone activity, it could be combined with Activities 4 and 5 as a short workshop or could form part of a larger programme on using the Uccello™ Process.

Aim of the activity

To help participants see how jumping to quick and easy solutions often leads to 'more of the same' and how, by suspending judgement even for a short time, it is possible to generate many more original and potentially successful ideas.

Group size

Approximately eight participants to one facilitator. The group should be split into sub-groups of four people.

Resources

Pens and paper for participants. Flipcharts.

Time required

30 minutes.

Process

1 The facilitator tells participants to work in their groups to try to suspend their judgement and to think 'out of the box' to solve a problem.

2 The facilitator reads aloud the brief for the business challenge on page 39 to the participants.

3 The facilitator instructs the groups to generate as many ideas as possible in ten minutes for how they might deal with the challenge facing the supermarket.

4 After ten minutes the facilitator asks each group to select from their ideas the one which they think is most likely to solve the problem. She then takes another example from each sub-group, this time asking them to select the one they think is their craziest idea.

5 The facilitator tells the group what the supermarket actually did and asks participants to what extent they were able to suspend judgement and how many of their ideas were simply variations on familiar things.

6 The facilitator leads a discussion about suspending judgement and draws out the following key points:

- People tend to go with their first thoughts and so don't push for more ideas. If they suspend judgement and push for more and more ideas they increase the chances of producing something genuinely new. (See Group Activity 1.)
- Sometimes quick solutions are necessary. When they're not, we can, by suspending judgement, generate more original ideas.

7 The facilitator asks participants what it felt like to really push their thinking and recommends that they try to remember this feeling so they can recreate it the next time they're generating ideas.

(See Chapter 3 for more information.)

Group Activity 7: New experiences

This activity, which further develops Step 2 of the Uccello™ Process, deals with collecting information and preparing our minds for creativity. It demonstrates how broadening our horizons, gaining new experiences and learning new things can stimulate our imagination and provide building blocks for creative thinking. It can be run as a stand-alone activity or as part of a larger programme.

Aim of the activity
To encourage participants to identify how they can gain new experiences and find new things to do that will stimulate their imagination and so provide material for their ideas generating sessions.

Group size
Approximately eight participants to one facilitator. The group should be split into sub-groups of four people.

Resources
Pens and paper. Flipcharts.

Time required
20 minutes.

Process
1 The facilitator introduces the activity with a brief talk on how experiencing new things and collecting information from diverse sources contributes to the creative and innovative process. He then asks the participants to work in their sub-groups to list as many different activities they could do that would stimulate their thinking and provide new experiences and information.
2 After ten minutes the facilitator asks each group for an example from the list they have produced. The other groups are instructed to do some 'magpie thinking' (see page 47) and note anything they hear which they could add to their own lists. The facilitator continues collecting examples for a further five minutes.
3 The facilitator asks participants to make a personal list of at least ten ideas which they could use themselves.

(See Chapter 3 for more information.)

Group Activity 8: Looking to the future

This activity follows on from Group Activity 7. It is designed specifically for use with the Uccello™ Process and should only be included as part of a workshop based around the Process. You can complete it whether you are a solo operator or are working in an organisation. It's essentially about collecting and categorising information.

Aim of the activity
To collect information about events, trends, innovations and new things that are happening in the groups' immediate environment and in the world at large which they can use when they start to generate ideas.

Group size
Approximately eight participants to one facilitator. The group should be split into sub-groups of four people.

Resources
Pens and paper. Flipcharts. Index cards in four different colours

Time required
One hour.

Process
1 The facilitator introduces the activity with a brief talk on how information forms the building blocks of the creative process. She comments on how, by combining diverse and unusual information, more imaginative results are produced. She asks each sub-group to identify and note on their flipcharts at least five or six things that are happening in each of the following categories:

- Their work group or organisation.
- Their industry or field of work.
- Other industries and fields of work.
- The world in general.

2 After approximately 30 minutes the facilitator asks sub-groups for examples from each heading and recommends that people take note of anything they think is interesting which they don't have on their own lists.

3 Individuals are told to keep their own lists as they will use them when they start combining information to generate new ideas. The facilitator gives out five or six of each colour of blank index card and advises participants to transfer each piece of information they want to keep onto a separate card using a different colour for each category.

4 The facilitator leads a discussion and asks the following questions:

  ▪ How many items on the lists produced are the same for each of the sub-groups?
  ▪ Why might there be so many similarities? Is it because the people in this group tend to use the same sources of information?
  ▪ What other sources could they use?

(See also Group Activity 7 above and Chapter 3 for more infor-mation.)

Group Activity 9: Experiment with your thinking

This activity deals with Step 3 in the Uccello™ Process and introduces the techniques we use as triggers to redirect our thinking. We often describe what we do in this activity as 'playing with our thinking' or 'standing our thinking on its head' because that's exactly what it feels like. Not only is it good fun but, during the activity, people quickly begin to get more creative ideas about how they might achieve their purpose. If they're going on to Step 6 of the Process they'll use these ideas to work with. This activity works well as a stand-alone workshop or as part of a larger programme.

Aim of the activity

To give participants the opportunity to practise using techniques for experimenting with their thinking and to experience how this triggers new and different possibilities.

Group size

Approximately eight participants to one facilitator. The group should be split into sub-groups of four people.

Resources

Instructions for using each technique. Flipcharts. Pens and paper.

Time required

One hour 30 minutes.

Process (Part 1)

1 The facilitator introduces the activity with a brief talk about experimenting with your thinking and why we need triggers to change the pattern of our thoughts and so open ourselves up to being more creative.

2 The facilitator explains to the participants that in this activity they will be using a number of different techniques for playing with their thinking and lists them on the flipchart and explains each one (see Chapter 4).

- 'Re-defining'
- 'Opposites'
- 'What's not there'
- 'Metaphor'.

3 The facilitator works with the whole group to agree a purpose statement which they will use to experiment with their thinking. This should be something that everyone can relate to and work with and could be the purpose statement they produced in Group Activity 2.

4 The facilitator outlines how each technique is used and participants are asked to take notes.

5 The facilitator tells groups that for the moment they will only be using the first three techniques and that each group will use a different one, i.e.:

- Group 1 *re-defines* the agreed purpose.
- Group 2 looks for the *opposite* of the purpose.
- Group 3 identifies *what's not there* currently in relation to the purpose.

6 The participants are instructed to spend the next 10 minutes using their assigned technique to experiment with their thinking in relation to their purpose. They should note on the flipchart any ideas they generate for feedback to the other sub-groups.

7 Each group is asked to share their ideas with the others and the thought processes they went through to produce them. The other groups are encouraged to ask questions to ensure everyone understands how to use each technique.

8 The facilitator asks everyone to select at least two ideas from those generated and tells them they will use these in the combining activity.

Process (Part 2)

9 The facilitator explains how using 'Metaphor' can help them experiment with their thinking (see Chapter 4).

10 Participants are instructed to spend twenty minutes with their sub-groups developing a metaphor for their agreed purpose.

11 The facilitator asks the groups to note their metaphor on their flipcharts so they can explain it to the other groups. He suggests that, if they would prefer to draw their metaphor rather than write it, they should do so.

12 After twenty minutes each sub-group talks through their metaphor and answers questions from the other groups.

13 The facilitator leads a discussion and draws out the following key points:

- Using any of the techniques acts as a trigger to redirect our thinking and so affects the way we view our purpose.
- Using these triggers can help us generate more imaginative ideas but we should not stop there, we need to combine these with other ideas and information to produce even more.
- Use at least two techniques in ideas generating sessions to produce better results. Choose the ones you like best.
- 'Metaphor' is possibly the most powerful of the techniques allowing people to think more imaginatively and to go on 'metaphoric excursions', i.e. explore the metaphor in some detail.

14 The facilitator asks participants to compare each of the techniques and comment on which they prefer and why.
15 The participants are told to keep a note of any ideas they generated during the session for using when they start combining.

(See Chapter 4 for more information.)

Group Activity 10: Relaxation

We can slow our minds down in many different ways and relaxing is one of them. This activity is a very effective way of demonstrating how to do it. Getting a large group of people to accept that it's ok to close their eyes and daydream is sometimes difficult, but it can be done. You can use this activity in a number of ways, either as a stand-alone activity or as part of a larger programme.

Aim of the activity
To give the group a method of relaxing which they can use when incubating ideas.

Group size
Unlimited.

Resources
Instructions for the activity (see pages 69–72). Music.

Time required
Ten minutes.

Process
1 The facilitator gives a brief introduction to incubating ideas and explains why it is an important part of the creative process.
2 The participants are reassured that this is nothing more than a relaxation activity; they will not be asked to do anything except relax and nothing bad will happen to them. The facilitator asks them to close their eyes, put their hands comfortably in their lap and place both feet flat on the floor then follows the steps outlined in Activity 5.1 on pages 69–72.

3 Once the activity is complete and everyone has opened their eyes, the facilitator allows a few moments for re-orientation before leading a discussion on the role of the unconscious in generating ideas. He highlights that, by slowing down our brainwaves, we can make connections and combinations we might not have otherwise made. The facilitator asks the group for examples of activities, other than a relaxation, that they could use to incubate ideas.

(See Chapter 5 for more information.)

Group Activity 11: Combining

This is the culmination of all the previous activities and results in people generating sometimes hundreds of ideas. It deals with Step 6 in the Uccello™ Process and is designed to be included as part of a larger programme in which the participants work through the process step by step. If you are working with a group who are either experienced in the Process or are already comfortable with combining and you don't want to conduct the whole programme, we would recommend that you first run Group Activity 8 to give them information to work with and possibly Group Activity 9 as a warm up. If they have worked through the whole Process they will already have an agreed purpose. If not, you will need to run Group Activity 1.

In our workshops, to add another dimension to the activity, we often ask someone in each small group to act as a 'banana person'. Their role, in addition to contributing to generating ideas, is to throw in 'a bunch of bananas' – a random word or phrase, unconnected to anything that is being said, that acts as a trigger to redirect the group's thinking or remove creative blocks, sometimes with surprising results (see page 62).

Aim of the activity

To give participants the opportunity to combine the information and ideas they have collected in order to generate ideas for how to achieve a real, relevant work-related purpose.

Group size

Approximately eight participants to one facilitator. The group should be split into sub-groups of four people.

Where possible, the groups should be made up of people who share a common purpose and who would benefit from the ideas generated.

Resources

Lists of information produced in Group Activity 8 (ideally with each one transferred onto a separate index card). Lists of ideas generated in Group Activity 9. Flipcharts, paper and pens. Masking tape or some other means of sticking flip chart pages to the walls. Music.

Time required

Two hours.

Process

1 The facilitator introduces combining as the essence of creativity. He tells the group that they will put together the information and ideas they've already collected with others to generate new ideas.

2 The sub-groups are each asked to write their purpose on their flipchart and to nominate someone who will act as scribe. (Note – a different person should take over as scribe approximately every 10–15 minutes.)

3 Each *person* is instructed to:

 ▪ Make a new list under a heading '*Blue sky ideas*'. This should contain anything which is interesting to the person and could include hobbies and interests – anything from music to sky diving, from knitting to taxidermy.

 ▪ Select one idea of their own which they generated in *Group Activity 9: Experiment with your thinking* and make a note of it.

 ▪ Select one item of information from the list they generated in *Group Activity 8: Looking to the future* under the category '*New things that are happening in the world*' and make a note of it.

4 Each *sub-group* is then instructed to:

- Take one set of the above information from one person in their sub-group, i.e. something from '*Blue sky ideas*', an idea generated in *Group Activity 9* and something from '*New things that are happening in the world*'. These three things should be written on the flipchart so that the whole sub-group can see them.
- Make three or four associations from each one and also note these on the flipchart.
- Combine any two items noted on the flipchart to make as many new ideas as possible that will meet the sub-group's chosen purpose.

5 Once each group has generated a few new ideas, the facilitator asks them to change to a different set of information from another member of their group and to repeat the three steps above.

6 The above three steps are repeated until the group has worked with information from each person in their group.

7 If this process is continued for approximately one and a half hours, anywhere between 50 and 150 ideas will be generated by each sub-group.

8 Each sub-group should stick their pages of ideas to the walls as they go along. (Reviewing them can often spark even more combinations and ideas.)

9 If the groups are not going to evaluate the ideas at this time, all the pages should be collected for use later.

10 Any debrief should be kept short and perhaps limited to asking the participants to comment on how the activity felt for them.

This activity generates a lot of energy as well as ideas and it's important that the facilitator maintains this momentum. We find that raising the tempo of the background music as the pace of activity increases often gives the groups a boost.

The participants will be tired after this activity and, while pushing them into another activity will not be productive, they need to know what will happen next and what they're going to do with all the ideas they have generated. The facilitator should ensure that the group arrange to meet again to evaluate the ideas and plan for their implementation.

(See Chapter 6 for more information.)

Group Activity 12: Evaluating ideas

This activity is about Step 7 of the Uccello™ Process where we move from creativity to innovation. This can be run as a stand-alone activity or as part of a larger programme. Although it can be done alone there is benefit in evaluating ideas with others because their different perspectives and values help to ensure balance and objectivity.

Aim of the activity

To give participants the opportunity to evaluate the ideas they have generated against a number of predetermined criteria so they can select one or more to take forward and implement.

Group size

Approximately eight participants to one facilitator. The group should be split into sub-groups of four people.

Resources

A copy of a decision grid for each participant. Pens and paper for participants. Flipchart pages of ideas generated during the combining session.

Time required

One hour.

Process

1 The facilitator introduces the activity with a short talk on evaluating ideas and the method the group will use.
2 Each group of four participants reviews all the ideas (not just their own) produced in the previous activity and agrees five that they think they can work with, at least one of which should be unusual and a riskier choice than the others, and which they think has the potential to meet their purpose.

3 Each member of the sub-groups enters the selected ideas on a decision grid and, working on his or her own, scores them.

4 Once the members of a sub-group have completed their decision grids they compare their scores with one another and discuss the differences until, ideally, a consensus is reached. The agreed sub-group scores are then entered on a 'master' decision grid and the final selection noted by each sub-group member so they can begin to make action plans for its implementation.

5 The facilitator leads a discussion about evaluating ideas and draws out the following key points:

   ▪ Having a set opportunity for evaluating stops people from limiting their ideas by prejudging them too early in the process.

   ▪ The headings on the decision grid are a guide and are specific to evaluating creative ideas.

   ▪ Although one idea may come out with a better score than others, this does not mean it must be implemented. The decision grid is only a way of organising our thinking.

(See Chapter 7 for more information on evaluating ideas and particularly how to build on ideas.)

Group Activity 13: Getting buy-in and managing resistance

Aim of the activity
To give the group a method of planning for how to get buy-in and manage any resistance to their idea.

Group size
Twelve to sixteen split into groups of four (ideally people who work together and who would benefit from planning together).

Resources
Flipcharts. A copy of Activity 8.1 *Getting buy-in* and a copy of Activity 8.2 *Managing resistance* for each participant.

Time required
45 minutes.

Process

1 The facilitator introduces the activity with a short talk on buy-in and the importance of careful planning if creative ideas are to become innovations.

2 Each work group completes Activity 8.1 *Getting buy-in* on page 111 in relation to their idea.

3 Once each work group has completed the four steps in planning to get buy-in, they should complete Activity 8.2 *Managing resistance* on page 113.

4 The facilitator leads a discussion and draws out the following key points:

- When plans fail the most common reason is lack of buy-in.
- To introduce a completely new idea to people whose buy-in is needed requires careful preparation and a planned presentation.
- For an idea to be accepted in an organisation it is important to demonstrate how it contributes to meeting strategic goals.
- An Ideas champion will increase the chances of success.

By now you will have worked through the whole Uccello™ Process and, whether you have done it with a group of work colleagues or friends, we hope you've experienced the different perspectives that other people bring to the creative and innovative process. Creativity is often seen as an individual activity and not something that can be done collectively. Our experience of working with groups and seeing the number and quality of ideas they produce convinces us that this is simply not the case. Creativity and innovation are as much group activities as they are individual pursuits.

Index